Sieges of the
Great Civil War
1642 – 1646

Sieges of the Great Civil War

1642 – 1646

*

PETER YOUNG &
WILFRID EMBERTON

BELL & HYMAN
London

First published in 1978 by
BELL & HYMAN LIMITED
Denmark House
37–39 Queen Elizabeth Street
London SE1 2QB

ISBN 0 7135 1983 5

Printed in Great Britain by
Ebenezer Baylis & Son Limited
The Trininy Press, Worcester, and London

In memory of
Margaret A. Middleton Emberton

Contents

Foreword

The battles of the Great Civil War of 1642–6 have captured the imagination of historians in plenty, while the sieges of the period have been largely neglected. This book was planned to fill this apparent gap. It does not pretend to be exhaustive. The limitations of space presented us with two choices, either to describe a large number of sieges very briefly or a select number fully. We decided that the latter course was the more useful, and have tried to illustrate several different types of siege operation.

Many gentlemen and burgesses, whether from loyalty or self-interest, chose to serve the King by pulling up their drawbridges or by slamming their gates and challenging the enemy to contest the issue. Some had little influence on the course of the war save to deprive the King's field army of the men who served to garrison them. Their numbers would have been sufficient to replace the army lost at Naseby had they taken the field at that time. But other strongholds, strategically placed and requiring but few defenders, were of very great value. Basing House and Donnington Castle, which commanded important routes, preying on military and commercial traffic, organising local contributions, and supporting friendly armies, are cases in point.

On the other side Parliament's occupation of Plymouth, Lyme and Taunton effectively paralysed the south-western Royalists at a critical stage of the war. Besides such major outposts other small garrisons held country houses or even villages and played their part; their raiding parties holding sway within a 10-mile radius – the distance a troop of horse could cover in a night, there and back.

Whilst it is obvious that maps are essential to the ready understanding of the event, we felt that something more than the usual maze of blocks, cryptic labels and lines was required, so that with the aid of our illustrator, Stephen Beck, we have contrived a type of picture map which we trust explains the action both convincingly and lucidly.

In writing a book of so wide a scope one becomes indebted to a large number of people, Borough and City officials, librarians, curators, property owners, and others who fall into none of these categories, who have responded readily and courteously to our quest for specialised local information. To name them individually, as they deserve, is impossible, but our appreciation is none the less genuine for the general form in which it is expressed.

P.Y.
W.J.E.

Chronology

1642	
July	
	First Siege of Hull
6	Portsmouth besieged by Waller
August	
22	King Charles raises his standard at Nottingham
September	
3	Southsea Castle taken by storm
7	Portsmouth surrendered by Goring
23	Skipton Castle besieged by Lambert
October	
23	BATTLE OF EDGEHILL
November	
13	The Confrontation at Turnham Green
December	
1	Farnham Castle taken by Waller
1643	
February	
27–9	Newark attacked by Ballard
April	
13	BATTLE OF RIPPLEFIELD
15–27	Reading besieged and taken by Essex
June	
18	ACTION AT CHALGROVE FIELD
July	
5	BATTLE OF LANSDOWN

13	BATTLE OF ROUNDWAY DOWN
	Chester besieged by Brereton who is later forced to withdraw
23–6	Bristol besieged and stormed by Prince Rupert
31	Attempt on Basing House
August	
10	Gloucester besieged by King Charles
September	
2	Hull besieged by Newcastle
5	Gloucester relieved by Essex
20	FIRST BATTLE OF NEWBURY
30	Plymouth besieged by Prince Maurice
October	
11	ACTION AT WINCEBY
12	Newcastle raises his siege of Hull
November	
7	Basing House besieged by Waller
15	Basing House relieved by Hopton
December	
22	Maurice abandons the siege of Plymouth
25	Pontefract Castle besieged by Lord Fairfax
1644	
January	
25	BATTLE AND RELIEF OF NANTWICH
February	
28	Lathom House besieged by Sir Thomas Fairfax
29	Newark besieged by Meldrum
March	
1	Second Siege of Pontefract Castle
21	Newark relieved by Prince Rupert

April

20	Lyme besieged by Prince Maurice
22	Leven and Fairfax besiege York

May

22	Essex relieves Lyme
27	Lathom House relieved by Prince Rupert

June

Rupert besieges and captures Liverpool

July

2	BATTLE OF MARSTON MOOR
11	Basing House besieged by Colonel Norton
16	Surrender of York
	Second Siege of Lathom House begins
31	Donnington Castle besieged by Lieutenant General Middleton

August

21	BATTLE OF LOSTWITHIEL

September

11	Basing House relieved by Colonel Gage
23	Basing House reinvested by Norton
29	Donnington Castle besieged by Colonel Horton

October

27	SECOND BATTLE OF NEWBURY
28	Donnington Castle besieged by Waller

November

9	Donnington Castle relieved
20	Siege of Basing House abandoned

December

2	Brereton besieges Chester
2	Surrender of Lathom House

1645

February

19	Chester relieved by Rupert and Maurice

March

1	Pontefract Castle relieved by Langdale
13	Maurice leaves Chester and Brereton resumes the siege

April

4	Formation of New Model Army at Windsor

June

14	BATTLE OF NASEBY

July

21	Pontefract Castle surrendered
23	Fall of Bridgwater

August

14	Fall of Sherborne Castle
20	Basing House besieged by Colonel Dalbier
23	Bristol besieged by Sir Thomas Fairfax

September

10	Bristol surrendered by Rupert
24	BATTLE OF ROWTON HEATH
28	Winchester Castle besieged by Cromwell

October

6	Winchester surrendered by Lord Ogle
14	Storm and destruction of Basing House
	Dalbier besieges Donnington Castle

1646

February

3	Chester surrendered by Lord Byron

March

30	Donnington surrendered by Sir John Boys

May

5	The King surrenders to the Scots
8	The King orders the surrender of Newark

June

25	The surrender of Oxford

1647
March

16	The surrender of Harlech Castle

Siege Warfare in the Seventeenth Century

In England 50 years of peace had rendered warfare a forgotten art, when, in 1642, the King raised his standard. 14 years earlier Sir Edward Cecil had declared that 'our old commanders both by sea and by land are worn out, and few men are bred in their place, for the knowledge of war and almost the thought of war is extinguished'.

In contrast the continental countries had long been at war developing new methods and tactics, while for the most part the island race slumbered. We say the most part, for the Englishmen who had chosen the profession of arms had sought a paymaster and tutor in the armies of Holland, Sweden, France, Denmark and even as far afield as Austria and Russia.

The Englishmen among them belong mainly to the Dutch school and the Scots to the Swedish. When they returned to this country upon the outbreak of hostilities there were not enough of them to go around, and many of the amateur soldiers and their equally amateur officers had perforce to learn their lessons by painful experience, before the survivors became the veterans of Marston Moor and Naseby. One of the specialised arts many of them had to acquire sooner or later was siegecraft. The development of the cannon had altered the whole concept of the method of reducing a stronghold. The mediæval castle with its lofty walls and towers dominated the scene for centuries, able to withstand enemy siege armies for months, even years. But when in 1453 the Turks, using cannon, breached the hitherto impregnable walls of Constantinople, a new era dawned.

Following the lead of the architects of the Italian Renaissance, Henry VIII's experts built strongholds of the new type, as for example at Southsea and at Hull, with low but immensely thick walls. Instead of tall imposing towers at the corners there were four-sided angular projections so designed that the artillery they mounted could sweep all the approaches in carefully planned relation to each other leaving no 'dead ground' in which an enemy might approach the base of the wall with impunity.

The Dutch designed a more economical type of fortification. They discovered that a suitably revetted wall made of earth and turf, provided it was of sufficient thickness, was a good substitute for masonry and if protected with timber palisades was just as difficult to surmount. That the continental veterans had absorbed these techniques is shown in the fortification of a dozen places, perhaps the prime example being the defences of Lyme which relied entirely on earthworks, the blockhouse walls being 12 feet thick and sometimes more.

What the belligerents lacked was not so much the experts – who were sedulously courted by both sides – but time to train and organise. Sometimes there was only time, as at Gloucester, to reinforce the mediæval or even Roman walls with a thick layer of earth to deaden the artillery shots. The mounds still existing against the walls of Warwick Castle clearly originated in the Civil War, and 'modern' gun ports can be seen in the mediæval fortifications on the north side.

While the methods of conducting a siege depended very greatly on the locality, the state of the ground, the type of stronghold, even the sympathies of the local inhabitants, the operations tended to follow a pattern. First it was necessary to create a fortified position, 'lines of circumvallation' as they were called, that would contain the fortress so that not only were the besiegers protected from the fire and attacks of the garrison, but they were able to prevent supplies, messengers or reinforcements reaching them.

The method was the age old one employed in Norman times and even earlier. A ditch was dug and the earth thrown inward, which, suitably revetted, became a wall. This could link, or have in association with it, various types of strongpoint as follows:

BASTION:	A large pentagonal fortification open at the rear.
REDAN:	Two faces forming an angle projecting forward of a wall.
REDOUBT:	A small square or triangular work closed on all sides.
HORNWORK:	An outwork having angular points or horns.
BREASTWORK:	A vague term for a temporary wall.
SCONCE:	A small fort.
OUTWORK:	A fortification outside, and independent of, the main line of fortification.

In their attempt to seal off the stronghold from the outside world the lines of circumvallation could cover some distance; in the case of Newark it was something like 14 miles.

The garrison, to keep them at a distance, or to strengthen walls considered too weak to stand against cannon fire, would often construct their own 'lines of countervallation', a good example being at Basing House where the south front was covered by earthworks and forts including fairly elaborate bastions.

Meanwhile the gunners would be occupied at this time in establishing batteries where they could play upon the defences with the most advantage. The gun positions would be made as economically as the rest by filling wicker baskets, known as gabions, with earth and other material, setting them up to form a protective screen. The area inside would be floored with planks, not for the gunners' comfort, but to save damaging the guns on the recoil. Traces of Civil War batteries can be seen at Lichfield and at Raglan Castle.

The two tables that follow may help to explain the organisation of the 'Trayne of Artillery', that 'sponge that could never be satisfied' as Clarendon called it.

Composition of the Trayne

1 General of Artillery
1 Lieutenant General
1 Comptroller
1 Commissary
10 Gentlemen of the Ordnance
25 Conductors
2 Comptrollers of Fortifications
1 Master Gunner
136 Gunners
1 Master Fireworker
2 Conductors of Fireworks
2 Battery Masters
1 Master Carpenter
12 Carpenters
1 Petardier
2 Waggon Makers
2 Gabion Makers
2 Harness Makers
1 Cooper
2 Farriers
1 Surgeon
1 Surgeon's mate
1 Captain of Miners
25 Miners
25 Pioneers
1 Trench Master
1 Waggon Master

who were supplemented by matrosses and waggoners.

The second table is based on the well-known one by William Eldred, 'Sometime Master Gunner of Dover Castle', whose exhaustive work, *The Gunners' Glasse*, must have been many a fledgling gunner's Bible. Other tables are given by Robert Norton, 'one of His Majesties gunners and engineers', whose book *The Gunner, showing the whole practice of Artillerie* was published in 1628, and by Robert Ward in his *Animadversions of War* in 1639.

Cannon in use in the Civil War

	Weight of shot	*Calibre*	*Weight of piece*	*Weight of charge*	*Maximum range*
CANNON ROYAL	63 lbs	8 ins	71.5 cwts	40 lbs	1500 yds
CANNON	47 lbs	7 ins	62 cwts	34 lbs	1740 yds
DEMI CANNON	27 lbs	6 ins	53.5 cwts	25 lbs	1600 yds
CULVERIN	15 lbs	5 ins	41 cwts	18 lbs	2000 yds
DEMI CULVERIN	9 lbs	4.5 ins	22.3 cwts	9 lbs	1800 yds

The list goes on to describe smaller guns right down to the little Robinet which threw a ¼ lb ball, but these would be, of course, little use for a siege.

It is estimated that the rate of fire of a Culverin served by an experienced crew would be about eight to ten rounds per hour. For battery the projectile would be roundshot, made of stone or iron. Caseshot, the modern equivalent of which is shrapnel, was useful in defence against a storming party, but would not, of course, do much damage to fortifications.

With the lines of circumvallation established and the artillery in position the next step was the construction of a number of redoubts in the no-man's land between the besiegers' earthworks and the enemy's fortress. From these a number of trenches would be dug in a zigzag fashion, creeping steadily towards the hostile defences. The engineers under whose direction they were constructed endeavoured to plan them so that they were safely defiladed from enemy fire. Gabions, filled as the trench was excavated, were arranged along the side which was towards the fortress.

The operation was carried out in this manner. First would come the leading sapper, whose expectation of life cannot have been great, pushing in front of him a well-packed gabion, laid horizontally, called the 'sap roller'. It was his job to make the first cut in the excavation and to plant the protecting gabions on the parapet. Other sappers followed him, deepening the trench and filling the gabions. Meanwhile the soldiers would construct small redoubts at intervals with a view to making the garrison keep their heads down with musketry and to provide covering fire in the event of a sally by the garrison.

Meanwhile the guns would be keeping up a heavy fire to ensure that the progress of the trenches was not impeded. Their purpose was to clear the rampart walks of the defenders, dismount their cannon and in general cause all the havoc possible.

Should the ground be too hard for deep excavation then a bank of earth would be raised on either side and a modicum of protection would be provided by 'blindes', that is bundles of brushwood or planks across the top. Where the ground was rocky and digging was impossible an approach way might be made of gabions pre-filled with earth and stones. Sometimes, as at Bristol (1643), the attacker had no alternative but to resort to storm tactics.

The task of the sappers was certainly no sinecure, for, as can be imagined, the nearer the trenches came to the walls the more concentrated the efforts to halt them. But supposing they had been successful in reaching the enemy's earthwork or ditch of the castle, what then? Usually a trumpeter or a drummer would deliver a final summons to surrender, probably the second or even the third. If this was accepted then commissioners from either side would meet to discuss terms. If the terms were unacceptable or the demand was rejected outright the third phase began. The guns would blast without ceasing, concentrating on that part of the wall or earthwork nearest to the end of the trench.

Few were the walls that could withstand the fire of the Cannon Royal. At Basing House its 63 lbs projectile battered the nine foot thick fortifications, toppling towers and walls, making wide breaches in 48 hours. Its fire directed against the walls of Winchester Castle made a gap 'large enough to march a regiment through'. Far more feared than the fire even of this giant cannon was the mortar, which lobbed a cast iron sphere packed with powder weighing up to 500 lbs (which was ignited by a separate fuse) high in the air, surmounting all obstacles.

The breach(es) having been made, the storm troops would race from the head of the trenches across the short stretch of open ground and attempt to carry the breach, and if successful the fortress was very likely to fall. It was the custom that if the defender caused the besiegers to storm, no quarter would be given, a fact which Cromwell underlined in his last ultimatum to the Marquis of Winchester before the fall of Basing House.

If, as at Boarstall, the ditch or moat surrounding the stronghold was wet, then the engineer's skill was taxed even further. Bundles of brushwood and bullrushes would have to be used to fill up the gap in the breach. Casualties on an operation of this sort were bound to be high.

Another mode of breaching was by mining: when the defenders could hear men working underneath them, they countermined. Sometimes they emerged into the besiegers' shaft and some bloody, close quarter work took place, but often they indulged in such schoolboyish pranks as letting a river in on the men below, or descending into the shaft and stealing the besiegers' powder before it could be exploded.

This then was the textbook siege. But many factors might modify its application. The services of an engineer of the calibre of Rupert's Walloon adviser, Bernard De Gomme, or the Parliament's hard-drinking Dutchman, John Dalbier, were not easy to obtain. Perhaps time was limited, or there was a strong possibility of relief, or perhaps the commander was fiery and impatient like Rupert or Fairfax. These were all factors that might drive the besieger to adopt methods far more direct than would seem admissible to their continental opposite number.

At Basing House, for example, the first major attack was mounted by Sir William Waller who needed a victory to restore his reputation after his rout at Roundway Down. Without any preliminary softening up he attempted to take the place by storm. He hoped to blow the gate in with a petard. This was a metal pot containing explosive attached to a board known as a 'madrier', which was meant to be firmly affixed to the enemy's gate. The petardier then fired the fuse. If it had been affixed correctly the lock would burst asunder. Like the sapper, the petardier could hardly expect to live to see his grandchildren. A typically English invention to cut down the mortality rate amongst petardiers was the 'sow', a long, low, wooden vehicle, loopholed for musketry, beneath which could be seen the feet of the crew hanging down, rather like the udders of a sow, hence the name, which was run up to the gate, and the petard was attached under cover. Owing to the determined resistance of the garrison, which was aided and abetted by the elements, Waller eventually withdrew, his reputation even more tarnished.

Next Colonel Richard Norton drew a 'starvation ring' around the House which came close to success and failed only because of outside intervention, first by Sir Henry Gage's relief expedition and secondly by the King's semi-victory at the second battle of Newbury.

The third and last, unorthodox, attempt on Basing was a combination of both the other attempts, storm and cannonade. This time it was stage-managed by two formidable commanders, Cromwell and Dalbier, and on this occasion there was no hope of relief. After a scientifically directed bombardment by the latter, the flood tide of the former's troops took the place in two hours. The siege had not perhaps been conducted strictly according to the textbook but none the less the end product was the same.

So far we have only dealt with the activities of the besiegers, but it is not to be supposed that the garrison assumed a passive role, sullen and defiant waiting for the *coup de grâce*. A mere glance through the following chapters will assure us that nothing could be further from the truth.

It is a well-known maxim that the best form of defence is to attack or, as Thomas Venn advised in his treatise, 'the first beginning is to keep the enemy from the town as far off and as long as you can. Therefore whatsoever without the works can put a stop to the enemy, the besieger [i.e. the besieged] must possess and defend as long as they can. They must use all their endeavour to hinder the approach of the enemy, therefore let them sally frequently, but warily lest they fall into snares to the irreparable loss of the town.' The garrisons of Newark and Gloucester both showed what a thorn in the flesh an active garrison could be.

Although we may feel that many Royalist garrisons might have been better employed in the ranks of King Charles's field armies, one cannot but admire the diehard spirit of some of them. The last to surrender, composed of only 42 officers and men, held out in Harlech Castle until 1647.

Today we can still see many traces of the siege warfare of the Civil War. Tangible evidence still remains, pieces of mortar shell in Lichfield Cathedral, musket holes in Alton and Basing church doors, a mortar at Hereford that actually bombarded Goodrich Castle, battery and breach at Raglan Castle; a rich harvest which may be gathered by the local historian, or indeed by anyone with a feeling for our heritage.

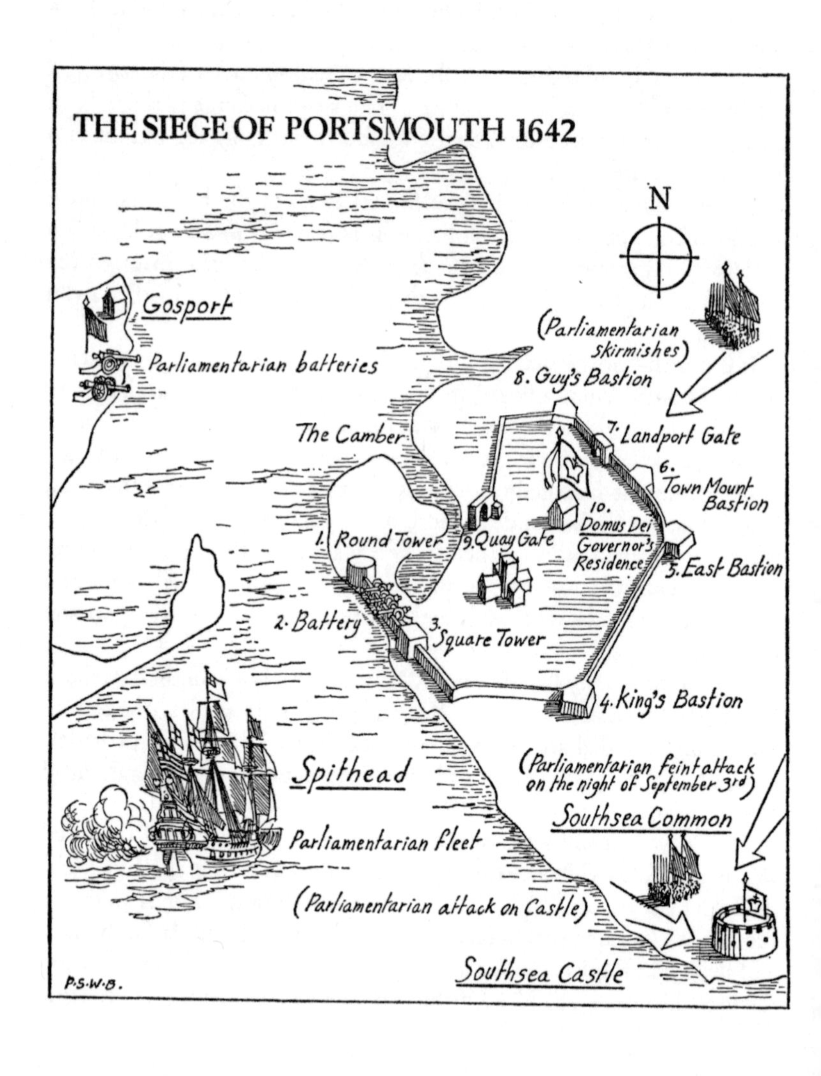
THE SIEGE OF PORTSMOUTH 1642
N
Gosport
Parliamentarian batteries
(Parliamentarian skirmishes)
8. Guy's Bastion
The Camber
7. Landport Gate
6. Town Mount Bastion
10. Domus Dei Governor's Residence
1. Round Tower
9. Quay Gate
5. East Bastion
2. Battery
3. Square Tower
4. King's Bastion
Spithead
(Parliamentarian feint attack on the night of September 3rd)
Southsea Common
Parliamentarian fleet
(Parliamentarian attack on Castle)
Southsea Castle
P.S.W.B.

Portsmouth

Defenders:	Town and Island: Lord George Goring (R)
	Southsea Castle: Captain Challoner (R)
Besieger:	Sir William Waller (P)
Duration:	6 August–7 September 1642
Outcome:	Town and Island, surrendered on terms 7 September
	Castle, taken by storm. Night of 3 September

At the outbreak of the Civil War Portsmouth was a small town – by modern standards a village – tucked away in the south-west corner of Portsea Island. From a map[1] of 1600, it can be seen that the surroundings were so sparsely inhabited that the dwellings of individual farmers are shown. The extent of the town can be said to approximate to the area enclosed by the modern St George's Road and half of Alexandra Road, then by a line sweeping south to bisect Pembroke Road, and slanting westward to the sea to enclose the Grand Parade. The thoroughfares of Lombard Street and Pembroke Road, High Street, St Nicholas Street, Penny Street, St Thomas Street and Oyster Street are all of some antiquity, being thus named in town maps of 1568 and 1668.[2] The original fortifications, commenced in the fourteenth century, were merely a simple encircling earthen wall[3] and ditch. War and the threat of war with France caused these primitive defences to be developed by Henry VII and Henry VIII, so that by 1545 they had become quite comprehensive. A painting[4] of the time shows strong battlemented walls with a rounded bastion at each corner and a massive gatehouse armed with cannon in the north face. Incorporated in the seaward defences are the Round Tower (finished *c.* 1426) and the Square Tower (1494), while to the east is the saluting platform originally constructed in the late fifteenth or early sixteenth centuries. This contains five cannon while others are seen on the rampart. Ships are seen anchored in the Camber which appears undefended, while a number of men are busily engaged in unloading a merchant ship on the quay.

Elizabeth I, who also feared an invasion, completely remodelled the fortifications. The rounded bastions at the corners were transformed into great half diamonds projecting forward of the curtain walls so that the ordnance they contained could provide a murderous cross fire. The eastern front was pierced by a further great bastion and a great, new bridge was built at the north end of town. The exposed western front was sealed by a stone wall with a strong gate guarded by two semi-bastions. When the monastic hospital of St Nicholas was acquired by Henry VIII, the buildings were used as an armoury, but in about 1580 they were converted for the use of the Military Governor. Nature also strengthened the defences, for in De Gommes's map the east front is covered by an expanse of boggy ground called the Little Marsh, while a small creek to the north had been dammed for the purpose of driving a mill, causing a considerable sheet of water labelled the Mill Pond.

By the time of the Civil War the country had been at peace for 70 years and the fortifications had fallen into comparative neglect. The only considerable part of the fortifications left today are those facing seawards, which retained their usefulness right up until the last war, while the landward defences lost their value in the middle of the last century and were virtually swept away by the town's expansion. When the Portsmouth Garrison was abolished in 1960 the seaward defences were acquired by the Corporation and restored as a rampart walk so that it is now possible to traverse almost the complete length of them with access to the towers and other buildings. Of interest to the Civil War student is the bust of Charles inset in the north face of the Square Tower with the inscription: 'After his travels through all France into Spain and having passed very many dangers both by sea and land he arrived here the 5th day of October 1623.'

Southsea Castle

The castle was one of a chain built at points on the south-east and south coasts by Henry VIII and was one mile to the east of Portsmouth town. For some three centuries it formed the key to the sea defences of Portsmouth Harbour. No vessel of any size could approach the haven without coming under its guns. Building was commenced in 1539 and a letter[5] to the King five years later tells of its progress: 'The state of your Highnesse's new fortress here, the which may be called a castle, both for the compass, strength and beauty and the device and fashion thereof . . . for the defence of your Majesties town and haven, as of the country hereabouts the like is not in the realm.' An engraving which depicts the attack of the French fleet on Portsmouth in 1545 shows the castle as having a great round keep, with star-shaped walls to the landward, but, facing the sea, a massive elevated platform with five great cannon mounted. It was destined to have an inglorious future. In March 1626 it was badly damaged by fire and it was obviously thought to be of so little importance that three years later it had not been repaired and was not even armed.

Walter James, the captain of the castle, wrote[6] bitterly that he had been ordered to 'lodge in a castle which is neither house or lodging, to guard a fort that is unprovided either for offence or defence and to maintain himself in the service of the state without receiving meat or money.' On 27 March 1640 another disastrous fire broke out and destroyed the lodging and ammunition rooms of the castle. Again the Captain, this time one John Mason, wrote a pleading letter begging that the Council of State might order the fortress to be repaired and furnished with ammunition, gun carriages and 'other habiliments of war' which had been certified as necessary two years previously. But the necessities of war change all things and on the eve of the Civil War we find that the castle,[7] which was surrounded by a wall three or four yards thick and about 30 feet high encircled by a moat five yards wide and three or four yards deep, was now mounting 14 guns, 12 of which were 12 pounders. It was held for the King by a captain named Challoner. Extensively remodelled in 1814, the castle is still intact and preserves very largely the Tudor plan. It has been adapted to serve as a museum illustrating the history of Portsmouth.

The Siege

Lord George Goring, Governor of Portsmouth, was a strange mixture of the engaging, unprincipled, devious scoundrel and gallant, impetuous soldier. Clarendon says bluntly 'on account of his private vices of drunkenness, cruelty and rapacity and of his political timidity and treachery scarcely anyone was more unworthy to be trusted . . . [yet] he was a person very winning and graceful in all his motions'. During 1642 Goring ran true to form, persuading both sides that he was loyal to them and accepting money from each, until on 2 August he called an assembly and declared his allegiance to the King. There were at this time,[8] of the ordinary garrison about 300 persons and of the townsfolk about 100 that were able to bear arms, and of Portsea Island, which was also under the command of the Governor, about 100 more. There were also some 50 officers and their servants and a further 50 horse.

With a speed the garrison found alarming the forces of Parliament started to gather on the slopes of Portsdown Hill. Almost immediately after Goring's declaration,[9] communication with the outside world was cut. On 10 August, Sir William Waller arrived with a troop of horse to take command of the assault force composed of trained bands from Hampshire, Sussex and Surrey. The same evening under cover of darkness, a bold Roundhead officer took a party in long boats into the heavily defended harbour waters and captured the only armed vessel the Royalists had (the *Henrietta Maria*), without a shot fired, and took her over to the other side of the harbour which was in Parliament hands.

Waller made no move until he judged he had sufficient strength. Then on the evening of 12 August, he struck at Portsbridge, the only access to the Island, and captured it. At this time[10] his force numbered 250 horse and 500 foot. With the enemy within striking distance, a number of skirmishes took place around and about the town walls. The lukewarm ardour of many of the garrison was further cooled by this and it became a nightly occurrence for soldiers to slip over the wall and run to Waller.

On 18 August they began to raise several batteries against the town at Gosport.[11] Despite the Royalists' attempts to dislodge them with cannon fire, within a fortnight these works had been completed and contained 12 pieces of ordnance. On 27 August Waller attempted to come to terms with Goring but was refused and the Gosport batteries opened fire. On 2 and 3 September, the Parliament gunners having apparently got the range, heavy damage was done in a 24-hour bombardment.

On the night of 3 September Southsea Castle was taken by storm. Properly equipped, garrisoned and stoutly defended, this could have presented an almost impregnable obstacle, but it contained only a dozen men, and the commander, Captain Challoner had been carousing with Goring that night with such gusto that he had to be roused from his bed to parley with the attackers. Asking to be left alone until the next morning, he went back to bed, upon which the men were ordered to scale the walls. As all the castle guns were trained on the landward side in anticipation of an attack from that direction, the storming party assembled on the sea shore and went over on that side. An eyewitness reported that Challoner, 'seeing himself nigh lost, demanded presently fair quarter, which he obtained with all his soldiers, though few in number beside his Lieutenant and Ensign'. Apparently Challoner did not feel his defeat keenly for he was soon drinking sherry with his captors, 'only desiring that three pieces of ordnance might be discharged' to let Goring know the castle was taken, which was answered by a furious connonade from the town. With this serious set-back Royalist morale declined still further and the Mayor and several officers deemed it time to escape over the wall. Early next day, 4 September, Goring called a council of war which decided to ask for a parley to discuss terms. During the negotiations he used as a strong bargaining counter[12] the vast quantity of powder (1400 barrels) in the garrison which he threatened to explode if the terms were unfavourable. The articles, containing 10 clauses, were finally agreed and on 7 September the Parliament troops took possession. Goring took boat to the continent whence he returned after several months, and such was his personal influence with the Queen that he was again given high command.

REFERENCES

1 By La Favelure (British Museum)

2 De Gommes's Map for the remodelling of the defences, 1668

3 Leland: 'A mudde waulle armid with Tymbre . . . having a ditche without it'

4 Source: an engraving by James Basire published in 1778, from a contemporary wall painting in Cowdray House depicting the attack of French fleet on Portsmouth in 1545

5 Anthony Knyvet, who styles himself 'Overseer of the Works', to Henry VIII, 22 October 1544

6 Walter James to Secretary Dorchester 17 January 1629, quoted in Corney, *Southsea Castle*, Portsmouth Corporation

7 See Gates, *Illustrated History of Portsmouth*, 1900, pp. 155–60

8 *A declaration of all the passages at the taking of Portsmouth*, 1642, (Portsmouth Central Library)

9 *Ibid*

10 *The Portsmouth Papers* No. 7, 10 Portsmouth City Council, 1969

11 *A declaration of all the passages . . .*

12 *Portsmouth Papers* No. 7, p. 20

Farnham Castle

Defenders:	Sir John Denham (R) Captain George Wither (P)
Besieger:	Sir William Waller (P)
Duration:	30 November–1 December 1642
Outcome:	Taken by storm

Farnham Castle suffered far less than many other castles that were actively concerned in the Civil War and has survived almost intact to this day. Being the possession of the Bishops of Winchester since the earliest times and conveniently situated as an overnight stopping place in their journeyings to London, the castle has been occupied and developed for 800 years. The earliest building on the site was built by Henry de Blois, the energetic brother of King Stephen, who erected a square tower on the usual motte in about 1138, with domestic buildings in a courtyard, the whole surrounded by an earthwork. Successive centuries saw these small beginnings blossom into a formidable fortress. De Blois' tower was demolished (though traces were found during excavations in 1958), and the entire mound was enclosed in masonry in the late twelfth century. In the fourteenth century the whole enclosure was surrounded by a high stone wall, pierced by towers on the line of the original earthwork.

Buck's *View* of 1737, made when the castle was in a state of neglect and disrepair, makes it clear that on the north and west fronts at least there were four, rather low, square towers while the shell keep itself was strengthened by great towers on the north, east, west and north-west. This keep was only slightly damaged on the south-east side during the Civil War and did not suffer extensive slighting. Entry to it was by a gatehouse consisting of two rectangular towers, dating probably from the thirteenth century. From the outside the keep appears intact, but inside the domestic buildings for the garrison have never recovered from the neglect of years during the Commonwealth and after. The Bishop's Palace (now a warm, centrally-heated college), the headquarters of Sir William Waller during the years 1643–4, owes a great deal to the restoration work by Bishop George Morley (1662–1684) who carried out extensive alterations and repairs. A memorandum in the British Museum notes that he spent £10640 on the castle. It is now a fascinating amalgam of Norman, Tudor and modern architecture, all of which play an equal part in the day-to-day life of the building. The Keep, which is in the care of the Ministry of Works, is open during the normal hours but the Bishop's Palace, being in private ownership, is open only at stated intervals.

The Siege

The story of the military operations round Farnham Castle could better be called a 'tale of two poets': gentlemen of opposing views and high ideals but with little conception of the realities of war. The first was a local landowner, George Wither (1588–1667), who held it for the Parliament despite the fact the town of Farnham and most of the local gentry were of Royalist sympathy. He occupied it on 14 October 1642 with two squadrons of volunteers, weak and ill-armed, with only 60 muskets between them. He had also raised a troop of horse, which bore the motto *Prorege, lege, grege* on its standard. Feeling that he was in a position of supreme importance he pestered Sir Richard Onslow for men, ordnance and military supplies. Onslow seems to have taken an opposite view and to have had a jaundiced opinion of the whole affair. With the advance of Rupert from Windsor to Egham the Parliament had more to trouble them than Farnham Castle, which they ordered Wither to evacuate on 8 November. Wither, feeling it was a stain on his honour, felt impelled to publish two pamphlets in defence of himself, *Se Defendendo* (1643) and *Justitiarus Justifacatus* (1646). Parliament, taking offence at the latter, promptly clapped him in jail.

The next amateur soldier to command the stronghold was Sir John Denham (1615–69), another poet, but also High Sheriff of Surrey. His defence of the castle for the King was indeed a sorry exhibition, the garrison being composed of 100 men. Sir William Waller 'with Colonel Fane and some others'[1] appeared before the castle and in the usual way summoned it to surrender. Seeing that they had brought no cannon, the Royalist commander thought himself safe enough and refused. But thereafter the garrison's courage seems to have evaporated, for without any apparent show of resistance they allowed the Roundheads to approach close enough to the gates to attach a petard and blow the gates open 'within the space of three hours'.[2] It might seem that a number of musketeers on the walls would have made it very costly for an enemy without artillery to achieve this. Before their hearts failed them, the garrison had placed 'great piles of wood which our soldiers had perforce to move',[3] but when the Roundheads entered, the Royalists 'threw their arms over the wall and begged for quarter'. Although this is the evidence of a Parliamentary writer, it is supported by Clarendon: 'they rendered it up with less resistance than was seemly' (1 December). For very little effort Waller had as his spoil £40000 in coin and plate, 300 sheep, 100 oxen 'besides some warlike provisions of powder and shot'.

After this, Denham was allowed to rejoin the King at Oxford, but one warlike experience seems to have sufficed him, for he retired into civilian life. When Wither was taken prisoner soon afterwards, Denham begged King Charles to pardon him on the ground that while Wither lived he, Denham, 'should not be the worst poet in England'.

REFERENCES

1 Vicars, *Parliamentarie-Chronicle*, 1643–4
2 *Ibid*
3 *Ibid*

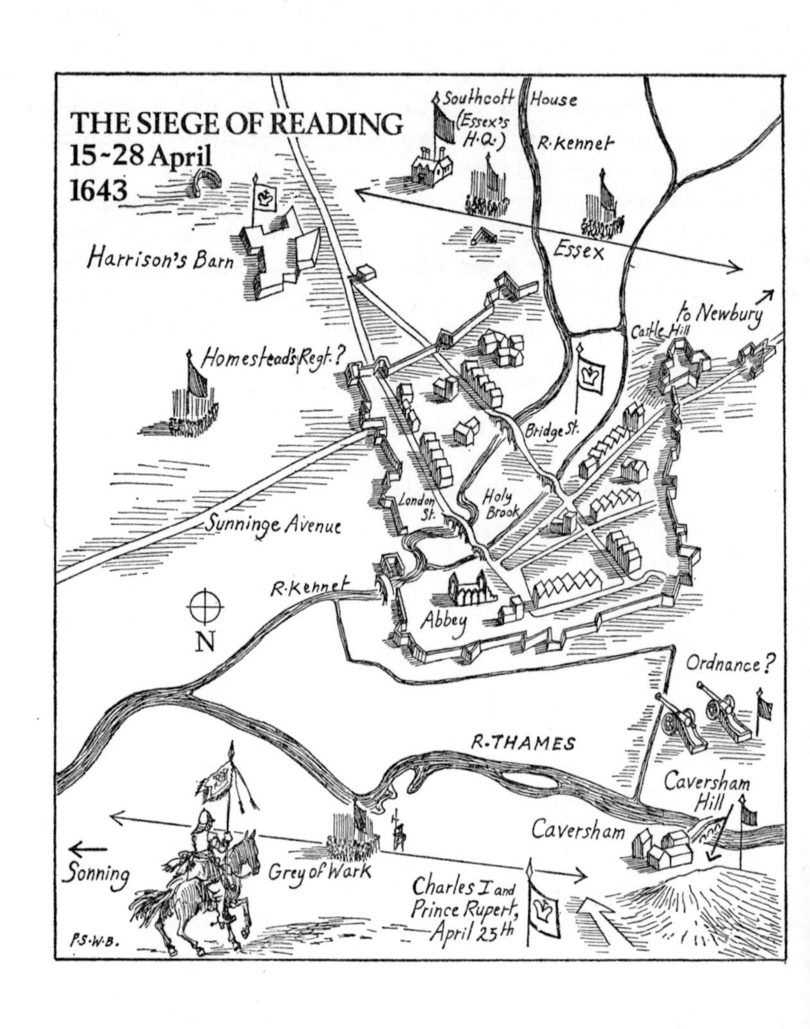
THE SIEGE OF READING
15~28 April
1643
Southcott House
(Essex's H.Q.)
R. Kennet
Harrison's Barn
Essex
to Newbury
Castle Hill
Homestead's Regt.?
Bridge St.
London St.
Holy Brook
Sunninge Avenue
R. Kennet
Abbey
N
Ordnance?
R. THAMES
Caversham Hill
Caversham
Sonning
Grey of Wark
Charles I and Prince Rupert, April 25th
P.S.W.B.

Reading

Defender: Sir Arthur Aston (R)
Besieger: Earl of Essex (P)
Duration: 15–28 April 1643
Outcome: Surrendered on terms by Aston's deputy, Colonel Richard Feilding, 27 April

During the Middle Ages the fame of Reading rested upon its Abbey; in fact it would be true to say the Abbey *was* Reading. Founded by King Henry II in 1121, the Abbey Church was said to have been the size of Westminster Abbey and its boundary walls to have extended north from St Laurence church at the juncture of modern Friar Street and the Forbury, turning right along Valpy Street and following Forbury Road along to the river. At the Dissolution of the Monasteries, the 31st Abbot, Hugh of Farringdon, was hanged over his own gateway in November 1539 with two of his monks, for refusing to yield up the monastery to the King's commissioners.

Today nothing remains of that great, spreading pile but the one great gateway and the Forbury Gardens which were the outer courtyard, although an engraving by M. Blackmore of 1759 shows a very great deal of the walls, above window height, still standing. There is supposed to have been a castle at Reading, of which, however, no archaeological evidence has ever been found. The names Castle Street and Castle Hill have come down to us, and indeed the latter occupies a suitably commanding site for a fortress. Leland concludes that a stronghold stood here in Saxon times and asserts that the Danes took possession of it in 871 but, of course, it would have not been a castle as the term is generally understood. Hearne[1] states that the castle was demolished by Henry II's troops coming from Wallingford who 'not only destroyed the castle of Brightwell but that which the King Stephen, contrary to all that was right and just, erected near the Abbey'.

Reading in the seventeenth century was a place of about 5000 inhabitants containing the nucleus of the present town with the majority of the street names remaining unchanged to this day, while the churches of St Laurence, St Giles and St Mary were all existing at the time of the siege.[2] Sir Arthur Aston had no enviable task in fortifying the town, and as no traces of the fortifications remain, it is fortunate that a map of them is preserved in the Bodleian Library, from which it would appear that they ran from the Abbey grounds to where the Abbey Bridge (now Blakes Bridge) stood. Apparently the River Kennet and its various channels constituted the defences until the earthworks recommenced on what might be supposed to be the line of the modern Watlington Street, then, bisecting Sunninge Avenue (the present A4), they continued on for several hundred yards and turned sharply north-west up Katesgrove Hill (commemorated now in the name of Kates Grove Lane) and halting at the Kennet again. The area between this and the Holy Brook are marked 'Drowned Meadows' and it is a matter for conjecture whether these fields were normally water-logged or whether the banks of the river were cut to flood this low-lying land, as in the defence of Oxford.[3] Beyond the Holy Brook the defences continued to a stronghold on Castle Hill and thence to the Church of the Grey Friars whose function was changed to that of a guard house. From there they turned at right angles past the Sheriff's house, parallel to Friar Street until they came again to the Abbey.

These works did not merely consist of straight lines of defences but contained all manner of field works from the simplest sort, called redans (two faces forming an angle projecting forward of the wall), to elaborate bastions at the corners. The nave of the Abbey was blown up to obtain stone to revet these works,[4] and the merchants' stores were raided for bales of wool to deaden the impact of the shot. In addition, various smaller advance posts were set to cover the principal roads, the biggest of which, called Harrison's Barn, was on Whitley Hill, covering the southern road that led to Basingstoke. Forward of the Castle Hill fort was another work named the 'Forlorn Hope' which commanded the Newbury Road.

The Siege

Strategically Reading was of the utmost importance. Not only did it lie almost half way between the headquarters of the two opposing factions, Oxford and London, so that its possessor had a convenient advance post from which to strike at the other, but it lay astride the main road from London to the west and also commanded the passage of the River Thames. It would seem that the citizens were neither for nor against the King and would much rather have been left alone to continue in their lucrative cloth trade, but the influential families in the area, the Knollys and Vachells, were connected with the Hampdens and so were Parliamentarian in outlook, as were the Blagraves (from whom the modern Blagrave Street takes its name), and in those days landowners controlled the destiny and hence the thinking of the large majority.

After the intaking of Brentford by Rupert on 12 November 1642, the King's victorious advance was stopped by the full force of Parliament's army drawn up in strong positions in the villages surrounding London, particularly at Turnham Green. Falling back from his capital, Charles arrived at Reading and stayed there long enough to repudiate the settlement terms proposed by Parliament in the last week of November. He then marched back to Oxford.

Charles left behind him as Governor Sir Arthur Aston, a professional soldier 'greatly esteemed where he was not known, and greatly detested where he was',[5] and a garrison of 2000 foot, a regiment of horse and four pieces of ordnance. Uncertain of the enemies' intentions, Aston had little time or materials to fortify the town, limited though its extent may seem by modern standards, but heartened when no immediate attack materialised he pursued the task with some diligence in the winter of 1642–3. The strength of the defences has been variously described by the Royalists (probably in extenuation of their defeat) as 'too mean to stand a siege, being intended for winter quarters, not a garrison'.[6] But Parliamentary sources state that the works were 'as tall as the houses, strongly fortified with a deep ditch round about'.[7]

But whatever their strength the testing time came on 15 April 1643 when Essex marched from Windsor and 'sat down before Reading'.[8] His forces consisted of 1600 foot and above 3000 horse. His artillery train included two heavy guns from the Tower of London. The Royalist garrison at this time was 3000 foot and a regiment of 300 horse. A council of war convened by the Parliament commander reached the decision[9] that it would be more profitable to besiege the town than assault it.

It is difficult to site the precise positions where the guns and troops were disposed, as few of the eyewitnesses agree, and some even make contradictory statements, but it emerges that Essex made his headquarters at Southcott (now Southcote) House, residence of Sir John Blagrave, and that his men blanketed the west front. Essex then summoned the town, to which Aston replied that he would sooner die or starve in it than surrender. Sir Samuel Luke states that the Parliament guns were sited by 16 April and they 'battered at it all the

16th day, they in the town playing on us both with their muskets and ordnance most fiercely'.

Soldiers got little rest on active service in those days, most of the work in siege warfare being performed at night. It can be seen that the methods used followed the general pattern. First the enemy stronghold was encircled, to exclude escape or outside help, then the approaches were made, each day creeping closer and closer. Luke gives a graphic account of the tightening noose. On 17 April he records that they were 'working both day and night on our trenches and advancing our lines' and on the 18th again 'all that night we spent in our approaches'. Before the ring finally snapped shut the garrison was further reinforced by 600 musketeers and 'several wagon load of ammunition'[10] which came up the river from Sonning. Essex gave the chief command of the approaches to Major General Phillip Skippon.[11]

There is some difficulty with the positioning of Lord Gray of Wark's force, for one Roundhead source describes him as 'near a strong outpost called Harrison's Barn' while another places him to the east. But Luke states positively that he 'appeared before the town with three regiments of foot . . . six troops of horse . . . two troops of dragoons and three pieces of ordnance . . . which begat the enemy about from Cawsom [Caversham] to Sonninge', and that is how he has been placed on the map. But Luke also says that the 'ordnance was on the south side betwixt two rivers called Kennett and Thames', which must be inaccurate as these rivers join to the north of the town. As the ground is rather higher in this direction and identification is so precise one may assume that he was mistaken in his bearings. Colonel Homestead's regiment of foot augmented by two troops of horse were 'set to watch the river front', from which it may be conjectured that he was stationed in that sector where the main town defence was the River Kennet.

On 19 April a curious happening occurred.[12] While Aston was 'in a court of guard near the enemy's work a cannon shot beat down a tile or brick which struck him on the head, and by the violence of the blow so stunned him that he was disabled'. Whether he was indeed struck dumb and dazed by the alleged blow so that he was unable to speak, or whether he foresaw the inevitability of defeat and wished the disgrace to go to another, hence this ingenious invention, may only be conjectured, but the command devolved into the senior Colonel, Richard Feilding.

On 22 April a servant of Sir Lewis Dyves, Flower by name, swam the Thames and gave the news that Rupert was coming to the town's relief and would attack Caversham Bridge. Unfortunately for him he was captured on his return swim and after 'questioning' revealed the intelligence, so that the Parliament outposts were alerted. That the town was under constant bombardment while the works crept closer and closer is seen from further entries in Luke's account: 'having advanced our ordnance to within pistol shot of one of their chief places' and 'we fell to battering the town' appears for 21 April.

By the time 25 April arrived, Feilding had had enough and asked for a parley. While negotiations proceeded, the forces of the King and Prince Rupert attacked Caversham Bridge[13] with forty colours of horse and nine regiments of foot. The Parliament forces made the 'hill so hot for them with our muskets that they were forced to retreat'.[14]

It seems that the attack was made after the truce had come into force from the accounts of both sides, and Colonel Feilding, being pressed by some of his fellow officers to attack from the town and thus take the Roundheads front and rear, plainly stated[15] 'that if the King himself should . . . command him to do it, he could not forfeit his honour and the faith he had pledged during the truce'. On the following day, 27 April, the articles of surrender were agreed, and the garrison marched out with the honours of war on 28 April. That the King did not approve of his conduct was apparent – and indeed it is somewhat difficult to see the necessity for such precipitate capitulation – for Feilding was court-martialled and sentenced to death for what we should term dereliction of duty. Twice he was led out to the scaffold, twice he was reprieved until at length he was pardoned.[16] But he lost his regiment and never again held command.

REFERENCES

1 Hearne, *Antiquarian Discourses*, 1771, Vol. 2, p. 188
2 See Speed's map, 1610
3 à Wood, *Life and Times*
4 Hinton, *A History of the Town of Reading*, 1954, p. 106
5 Clarendon, Vol. V, p. 120
6 *Ibid*
7 *Perfect journall of the daily proceedings of that memorable Parliament*, 10 February
8 Clarendon
9 *Ibid*
10 Luke, *Journal*, ed. Phillip, 1950

[11] *Special passages* No. 17. According to *Perfect Journall* . . . however, Gray was on the south side
[12] Recorded in Coates, *History and Antiquities of Reading*, 1832, p. 27
[13] Luke
[14] *Ibid*
[15] *Ibid*
[16] Clarendon

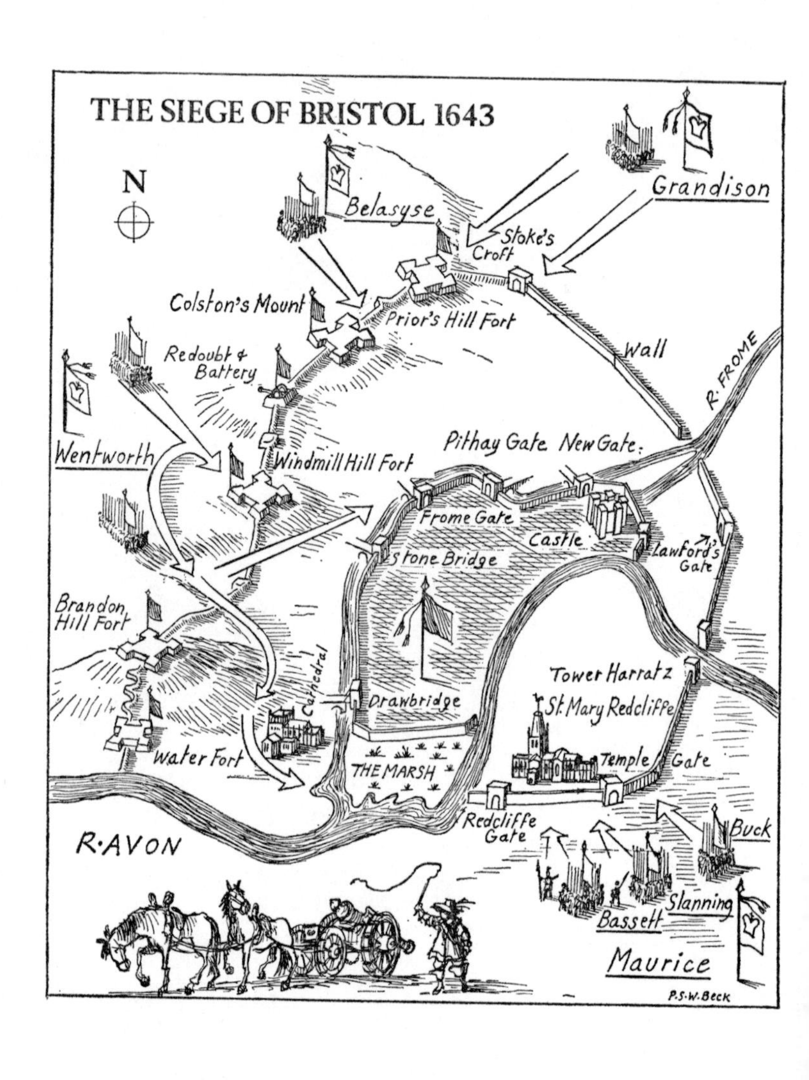
THE SIEGE OF BRISTOL 1643
N
Belasyse
Grandison
Stoke's Croft
Colston's Mount
Prior's Hill Fort
Wall
R. FROME
Redoubt & Battery
Wentworth
Windmill Hill Fort
Pithay Gate
New Gate
Frome Gate
Castle
Lawford's Gate
Stone Bridge
Brandon Hill Fort
Cathedral
Drawbridge
Tower Harratz
St. Mary Redcliffe
Temple Gate
Water Fort
THE MARSH
Redcliffe Gate
R·AVON
Buck
Slanning
Bassett
Maurice
P.S.W. Beck

Bristol

Defender:	(1) Colonel Nathaniel Fiennes (P)
	(2) Prince Rupert (R)
Besieger:	(1) Prince Rupert (R)
	(2) Sir Thomas Fairfax (P)
Duration:	(1) 23–26 July 1643
	(2) 23 August–10 September 1645
Outcome:	(1) Surrendered on terms after being stormed
	(2) Surrendered on terms after being stormed

As it grew up round its harbour, Bristol seemed from the beginning to be destined for prominence, and by the seventeenth century it was the second most important city and port in the Kingdom. The Rivers Frome and Avon formed a moat round two sides of the city, leaving only a relatively narrow gap to the east. The castle, first mentioned by Symeon of Durham in 1088, was designed to seal this gap as a cork in a bottle, and by the time of the Civil War was a very great place indeed.

Major Edward Wood[1] giving evidence at Nathaniel Fiennes trial, described it as 'a very large stronghold, fortified with a very broad deep ditch, in part wet and dry, having a very good well in it', and went on to describe it further: 'The castle stood on a steep lofty slope, that was not mineable . . . it [being] built on solid rock . . . the foot of the castle upon a mount or rampart was fortified with a gallant parapet wall flanking . . . at the base being, as I guess twelve feet thick. The walls . . . were very high, well repaired, and stored with strong flanking towers and galleries on the top. Within . . . was an exceedingly high fort or tower that commanded both fort and town . . . [which] I am sure had been past the power of cannon to batter . . .'

Recent excavations have proved that this keep (or tower, as Wood described it) was indeed a mighty edifice, the walls being 17 feet thick, the whole being estimated to have been roughly the size of the White Tower in the Tower of London. Today it is difficult to realise that this great stronghold covered 18 acres or twice the area of Caernarvon Castle.

John Smith's map of Bristol dated 1568 shows typical mediæval walls studded at rather wide intervals by squat towers enclosing not only the old city but the commercial suburb of Redcliffe that had overflowed across the Avon until it was almost a town in its own right. Also shown is the great stone bridge connecting the two communities. Apparently there was a disadvantage in living in the 'better part' of town for, when the cost of the defences came to be met, the residents of Redcliffe were required to pay for their own wall, but in the old town fortification was financed by a co-operative effort by the citizens on both sides of the river.

When the Civil War broke out the defences were implemented by a broader circle of fortifications. These were composed of five forts, all self-contained with dry ditches and palisades surrounding them. They were connected by an earthwork about five feet high and three feet thick at the top. Outside was a ditch six feet wide and about five feet in depth. In places, owing to the rocky ground, however, the ditch was very shallow, but round the forts, with the exception of Brandon Hill, it was eight or nine feet deep.

About 800 yards from where the Frome joined the Avon the curtain wall turned north up to Brandon Hill Fort, from there it descended slightly, then ran up to Windmill Hill Fort, continuing on to a redoubt and battery sited on St Michael's Hill. North-east stood another fort, Colston's Mount, which in turn was flanked by Priors Hill Fort, the northernmost point of the defences. From there the wall ran down to rejoin the Frome and link up with the other defences at Lawford's Gate. Formidable as they may seem, these defences needed a great number of men to man them adequately, and Bristol was to prove a great wrecker of military reputations.

The Siege

The decisive nature of the battle of Roundway Down near Devizes removed the Roundhead threat to Oxford for the time being, and the King's Council of War were quick to seize the opportunity to complete the conquest of the West. On 18 July 1643, Prince Rupert set out from Oxford with a formidable force. He had three brigades of infantry under Colonel General Lord Grandison, Colonel Henry Wentworth and Colonel John Belasyse. His two wings of horse were commanded by Major General Sir Arthur Aston and Colonel Charles Gerrard, with nine troops of dragoons under Colonel Henry Washington. There is some doubt as to their exact numbers: Clarendon gives a total of 14000 men while others as many as 20000. Fiennes contents himself by estimating 15 regiments of foot and 12 of horse. Monsieur de la Roche and Captain Samuel Fawcett commanded the artillery train.

Arriving at Bristol on 23 July the Prince lost no time in carrying out a reconnaissance in the afternoon from Durdham Down. To man the defences, Colonel Nathaniel Fiennes had 300 horse and 1500 foot,[2] with an indeterminate number of townsmen; a very small number to hold a three-mile front. Spread out round the broad circumference of the defences were 100 guns.

Next day Rupert summoned the city and, when Fiennes defied him, commenced his preparations. To the south of the town his brother, Maurice, with the Western Army, began constructing batteries. On 25 July the Prince crossed the River Avon and held a council of war with his commanders. The decision they had to make was whether to storm, or to use the time-consuming methods of the leaguer. According to Colonel Walter Slingsby the council was fairly evenly divided, the Western officers preferring a formal siege, while Rupert's officers, imbued with his taste for the most direct method, were for taking the town by escalade.[3] Apparently there was some kind of casting vote for we are told that 'Prince Rupert prevailed with his brother and it was then resolved on a general assault'. But in any case the rocky nature of the terrain made it practically impossible to approach the line of defences by parallels and trenches.

This course decided on, preparations were soon put in hand. The assault was scheduled for daybreak the next morning, the password 'Oxford', the field sign the wearing of green colours. The signal for the general assault was to be the firing of two demi-cannon from Grandison's battery. Thereafter the brigade commanders were 'to play it by ear'. The Cornishmen, no doubt having had enough of the nerve-stretching tension, started their attack long before daybreak. In other words, they 'jumped the gun'. There was no stopping them, so Rupert gave the prearranged signal for the assault.

Grandison's brigade valiantly assailed the two forts in their sector, Stokes Croft and Prior's Hill, but had ill-fortune. A petard affixed to the gate of the former insufficiently damaged the bolts. Penetrating to the very ditch of the fortifications, the Cavaliers were eventually beaten off, leaving the ditch full of casualties and their young leader mortally wounded. Belasyse had even less success. Lacking ladders, his men found the walls unscalable and took refuge behind a stone wall, some few retreating out of the hot fire. Rupert had his charger shot under him while attempting to lead them back.

But the results were not all negative. Wentworth's tertia (a term for an indeterminate number of regiments, the modern equivalent being brigade), whose objective was the area between Brandon Hill and Windmill Hill Forts, had to advance over rough ground, where they were unable to maintain their formation. Into the broken mass the Roundhead gunners and musketeers poured a heavy fire, but instead of retreating, the Royalists ran forward and found that once up against the works, they were almost invisible from the forts, that is to say in dead ground. Thus fortuitously protected, and well-led by their colonels, they hurled grenades over the earthworks and on scaling them saw the defenders streaming back towards the town. The attackers let them go and attempted to demolish the barrier to admit the horse. Parliamentary cavalry, posted at this point to prevent this happening, for some reason failed to charge, and when eventually Fiennes' own horse counter-attacked it was too late, for 300 of the enemy were over and a blast of musketry hurled them back. Reforming, they charged again and were met with fire pikes which the horses would not stand.

The Western Army attacking on the southern front were driven back with very heavy losses. They had scaling ladders and faggots, thanks to the foresight of Prince Maurice, but a fanatical defence repulsed them time and again. When they retreated for the last time, it was found that of the three tertia leaders, Colonel Brutus Buck, Sir Nicholas Slanning and Major General Bassett, only the last named had survived, badly wounded, as was Sir Bernard Astley.

The fight had been raging for 14 hours when, more by luck than judgement, Wentworth's men took a strongpoint called 'Essex Work'. Consolidating this, they were eventually joined by some horse under Aston's and Belasyse's brigade of foot. Wentworth then advanced upon College Green, and towards the Quay, while Belasyse, supported by Aston, assaulted the Frome Gate. The fight raged for another two hours, the garrison swarming out under covering fire from the windows, while even the women laboured to construct a bulwark of earth and wool bales inside the gate.

The carnage here was terrible. The gallant Colonel Henry Lunsford fell, shot through the heart; Belasyse himself had a head wound and it seemed that exhaustion would have compelled the Royalists to fall back, had they not been reinforced by some of Grandison's tertia which drove the defenders back into the town. Rupert had established his headquarters within the breach where he could control operations.

Determined to strengthen his foothold, he sent to Maurice for 1000 of his Cornishmen. But the fight was over. Fiennes, who, with an inadequate force, had fought hard to defend a city whose wealthier inhabitants at least were hostile to him, sued for terms, which were agreed upon by 10 o'clock that night: 'those articles which were most disadvantageous to the garrison having been settled by Fiennes alone as he walked in the garden with Colonel Gerard who negotiated for the Prince.'

When Fiennes returned to London he was court-martialled for his allegedly premature surrender and sentenced to death, but was reprieved by Lord General Essex's order – proof of the old nobleman's good sense and generous heart.

The second siege was something of a carbon copy of the first with the parties reversed. By August 1645 the tide had set against the Royalist cause. All but the most optimistic or obtuse could see the writing was on the wall; even Rupert had urged the King, albeit in a somewhat roundabout fashion, to make what terms he could with his opponents. But the King was adamant and so the war went on. Rupert was now Governor of Bristol. Bridgwater fell to the New Model Army on 23 July, Sherborne Castle on 14 August. It was now the turn of Bristol, the chief stronghold remaining to the Royalists in the West. Sprigge puts its value concisely: 'it is the only considerable port the King has in the whole of Kingdom for shipping, trade or riches.'

Ireton was sent ahead with 2000 horse and dragoons 'to preserve the towns adjacent to Bristol from plunder and firing for the better accommodation of our quarters'. Captain Moulton was ordered to bring warships round from Milford Haven to blockade Bristol from the sea. On 22 August there was a 'general rendezvous of horse and all that day was spent in the setting of guards on the Somerset side', the next day being also spent 'setting quarters and guards on the other side of Bristol'. Rumours were rife at this time that the King was on his way to join Goring in an attempt to relieve the city, rumours which seemed to be confirmed when Goring's letters were intercepted saying that he would be prepared to assault the besiegers in three weeks' time. Sprigge also notes that 'further advertisements confirmed our former hints of the King's advance from Oxford towards Bristol.'

At noon on 1 September, Rupert made a sally, in wet and misty weather, with 1000 horse and 600 foot, but was beaten back by the horse and foot of Colonel Rainsborough's brigade. The continued rumours of the approach of a relief force no doubt precipitated a council of war at which, in their turn, the Roundhead commanders had to decide between siege or storm.

Once again, the direct course was chosen. Sir Thomas Fairfax posted a brigade of horse on Durdham Down consisting of Ireton, Butler and Fleetwood's regiment to prevent relief or escape. Weldon's brigade was to assault from the south in the same area that the Western Army had battered. Four regiments of foot under Rainsborough were to be launched against Prior's Hill Fort and the wall between it and the River Frome. The signal for the general assault was to be the lighting of a huge bonfire and 'the firing of four great guns against Prior's Fort'.

Sprigge lists the successes of the assault as follows:[4]

'Colonel Montague and Colonel Pickering with their regiments at Lawford's Gate entered speedily, and recovered 22 great guns and took many prisoners . . . Major Desborough advancing with the horse after them, having the command of the General's regiment, and part of Colonel Graves.'

'Sir Hardress Waller's and the General's regiments commanded by Lt. Col. Jackson entered between Lawford's Gate and the River Froom.'

'Colonel Rainsborough and Colonel Hammond's regiments entered near Prior's Fort.'

'Major General Skippon's and Colonel Birche's entered nearer to the River Froom.'

'The regiment commanded by Lt. Col. Pride was divided; part assigned to the service of Prior's Fort, and the rest to alarm the great fort, and afterwards they took a little fort of Welchmen.'

Once again the line of defences failed to hold and the pioneers broke down the barricade to let in the cavalry, who were charged by Royalist horse under Colonel Taylor, who was mortally wounded. His loss so demoralised the defending troop that they fell back on Colston's Fort and did not charge again. Prior's Hill Fort kept firing for two hours after the line was pierced. Although the scaling ladders were found to be too short, the Parliamentarians at last fought their way in, a certain Captain Lagoe of Pride's regiment being the first to seize the Royalist Colours. So enraged were the attackers that they refused to give quarter, killing Major Price, the Welsh commander, and others, until their officers got them under control. Four hours after the fort fell Rupert sent a trumpet and Fairfax agreed to parley. On 11 September the Royalists marched out with 500 horse and 1000 foot, Fairfax providing an escort for two miles along the way to Oxford.

News of the surrender came to King Charles at Raglan Castle. It was a shattering blow. Bristol destroyed two military reputations, Fiennes' and Rupert's, for although the Prince was not put on trial for his life his uncle wrote him a bitter letter revoking his commission and adding,[5] 'I must remind you of your letter of 12th August, whereby you assured me that if no mutiny happened you would keep Bristol for four months. Did you keep it four days? Was there anything like a mutiny? My conclusion is, to desire you to seek your subsistence . . . somewhere beyond the seas, to which end I send you herewith a pass . . .'

REFERENCES

1 *Memoirs of Bristol*, S. Seyer, 1823, Vol. II, p. 301

2 See Young and Holmes, *The English Civil War*, 1974, p. 141

3 Slingsby's *Relations*, in Hopton, *Bellum Civile* 1642–44, ed. Healey, 1902, p. 92

4 Sprigge was Chaplain to Sir Thomas Fairfax to whom he dedicated his book *Anglia Redivira*

5 Clarendon, IX, p. 90

THE SIEGE OF GLOUCESTER
1643
St. Oswald's Church
Kingsholm
The Worcestershire Forces
Vavasour
Alney Island & the Vineyard
The Cathedral
North Gate
Northgate street
The High Cross
West Gate
Westgate street
Astley
East Gate
The Quay
The Castle
Southgate street
The Oxleaze
Half Moon
Greyfriars
R. SEVERN
Ordnance
South Gate
Lord Forth
Gawdy Green
Llanthony
N
Charles I
Foot and Ordnance
P.S.W.B.

Gloucester

Defender:	Colonel Edward Massey (P)
Besieger:	King Charles I (R)
Duration:	10 August–5 September 1643
Outcome:	Relieved by the Earl of Essex (P)

Like so many other English cities Gloucester was founded by the Romans as a military base and fortress. Realising its strategic importance as the lowest practicable crossing of the Severn, they constructed a legionary fortress where in due season the Twentieth Legion and, later, the Second Augusta were stationed. The town that grew up round it was named Glevum.

Despite the devastation caused by the Saxons in the sixth century there is much about Gloucester's main street plan that recalls its Roman past, the roads crossing en route to gates, long since demolished, at the four points of the compass. The glory of Gloucester is its Cathedral, built between 1089 and 1128. After the interment there of the murdered King Edward II in 1327, the east end was remodelled, the internal face being lined with masonry in the Perpendicular style. The east window, installed to commemorate Edward III's victory at Crécy in 1346, is 72 feet by 38 feet, the second largest of its kind in the country. The cloisters rebuilt in the fourteenth century contain the earliest known fan vaulting. It is fortunate that 'while others suffered from the ravages of the Parliamentarians [it] was preserved from serious mutilation even in the hands of spoilers and in a desolating age'.[1]

Speed's map 'which does not profess to give an exact representation'[2] shows that the citizens, as in the majority of other towns, had busied themselves in the pleasant task of accumulating profits, never supposing that they would ever need any defences for the city. So that when the need came, there was little of the ancient walls still standing. In summing up, Washbourn gives a description of what remained to protect the city as follows:

West and North	From the Westgate Bridge at the Severn to the Lower or Outer North Gate	No walls. A small work. In front marshy ground.

North-east and East	From the lower North Gate to the East Gate	A slender work upon a low ground as far as the postern gate where there was a turn southward and from that point to the East Gate the ancient walls.
East and South	From the East Gate to the South Gate	The ancient walls but nothing to flank the enemy's approach.
South and West	From the South Gate to the West Gate	As far as the Castle chiefly a strong and lofty work, a breastwork by the river side under the Castle, on the quay a half-moon covering the river.

The castle is mentioned in the Domesday Survey and it appears that the 'Kings Tower', probably the keep, was in existence *c.* 1108. Work was done on it in 1129–30 and again in 1158–9. More of the castle works were mentioned in 1172–4, with extensive repairs to the walls, including a 'tower over the gateway . . . and the bridge' in 1184. For a century after the siege by Prince Edward in the Barons' War in 1263, the keep was derelict, but it evidently underwent repair, for in the fourteenth century a sketch depicts a crenellated tower, three storeys high, with turrets rising above the walls. Speed's map shows first a circular wall with a low gatehouse in the north face and in the centre of the enclosure a building that has the appearance of a thirteenth century great hall. The remains, south-east of the Cathedral, were destroyed in 1791.

The Siege

With the great activities in the West during 1643, it must have seemed obvious to the authorities of Gloucester that it could not be long before they were visited, so they looked to their defences, probably for the first time since the Wars of the Roses, and found 'the city was open on three parts'[3] and thereupon 'the citizens did mainely show their care and affection in fortifying the town', but still regretted the necessity, finding the work 'both expensive and tedious'. It would seem that many of the merchants, who parted unwillingly with their gold, were unconvinced of the necessity, for they little thought that the 'cloud of blood should be blown from the north and settle over us, over whom it afterward brake in so many showers'. But with the surrender of Bristol (26 July 1643) little doubt remained either of the need for defences or the likelihood of assault.

Preliminaries started very soon after this. Alderman Purdy, one of the Gloucester M.P.s, received a letter from the Royalists on 4 August, advising the surrender of the city and enumerating the strength of the King's Army – all Rupert's force, plus 2000 Welsh clubmen (who would presently be armed from the Bristol arsenal), 1500 armed Welshmen, 800 foot, a regiment of horse from Worcester, and so on.

The following day it was reported that 2000 enemy horse were within 10 miles of Gloucester, which caused messengers to be sent at horsekilling speed to Westminster.[4] The first contact with the enemy came when Captains Purdy and Evans, hearing of Royalist foragers at Tuffleigh, issued out to check them, and, finding the place empty, followed on to Brockthorpe (three miles out) where they had a small skirmish, returning back on the city without hurt. On 10 August, the King 'with about six thousand horse and foot, as we conceived . . . faced us in Tredworth Field . . . about a quarter of a mile of town', while another 'two thousand horse faced us at Walham' (NNW of the city).[5]

Somerset Herald presented a formal summons to surrender during the course of that afternoon.[6] 'Out of our tender compassion to our City of Gloucester, and that it may not receive predjudice by our army, which we cannot prevent, if we be compelled to assault it, . . . we are gratiously pleased to let all the inhabitants of, and all persons within the city . . . know that if they shall immediately . . . submit this city to us, we are contented to freely and absolutely to pardon every one of them . . . But should they neglect this offer . . . they must thank themselves for all the calamities and miseries that fall upon them . . .'

After some debate, the following reply was drafted and presented by Major Pudsey accompanied by Tobias Jordan (Sheriff of Gloucester in 1644) as representatives of the civil and military authorities.[7] Clarendon describes them as men of 'lean, pale, sharp and bad visages' who delivered their reply 'without any circumstance of duty or good manners, in a pert, shrill, undismayed accent'. 'We, the inhabitants, magistrates, officers and soldiers, within this garrison of Gloucester unto his Majesties gracious message, return this humble answer. That we doe keepe this city according to our oathes and allegiance . . . and doe accordingly conceive ourselves wholy bound to obey the commandes of his majestie, as signified by both houses of parliament, and are resolved by God's helpe to keepe this city accordingly.'

On receipt of this defiant message, the Royalists made an assault both from the east and west but the garrison had taken the precaution of firing the suburbs and the attackers were 'fired out'. One house in Barton Street (an extension of Eastgate Street) was unconsumed and formed a shelter for the musketeers before they were dislodged by cannon fire. The rest of the day was spent by the besieged in cutting turves to repair the defences, Edward Massey the Governor deciding that the two sconces on Alney Island and at the Vineyard should be abandoned for lack of men, 'we being not above fourteen hundred at most'. Corbet enumerates the garrison more precisely:

'Two regiments of foot, a hundred horse with the trained bands, and a few reformadoes: there were besides about an hundred horse and dragoons from Berkley Castle, in the whole about fifteen hundred men; forty single barrels of gunpowder, with a slender artillery.'

At daybreak the defenders found that the Royalists had not been idle for 'the enemy had . . . begun their entrenchments at Gawdy Green'[8] on the south of the city 'and about Issolds house on the east part', both within musket shot of the defences. The water supply had also been cut and the course of the stream that drove the city corn mills diverted, 'leaving us to content ourselves with pumpe and seaverne water and to grinde our corne with horse-mills'.[9]

About 13 August, leaving a guard at the Vineyard, Colonel General Sir William Vavasour and his Welshmen crossed over the Severn by a bridge of boats to join the newly-arrived troops from Worcester at Longford and Kingsholm on the north-west side of Gloucester where they camped less than half a mile distant. With Lord Ruthven encamped at Llanthony close to the city wall and Sir Jacob Astley quartered in Barton Street, the encirclement was complete.

While all this activity was proceeding, the garrison, 'perceiving by there cannon baskets they placed in their square redoubt at Gawdy Green, that they [the enemy] intended a battery there', began to strengthen the 'town walles from the south to the east gate' with earth to a great depth.

On the same day the bombardment opened with this same battery pounding the walls with 15 and 23 pound shot, apparently quite effectively, for Dorney notes that next day 'we quickly made up the breach with woole sacks and cannon baskets'.

At this stage, both parties were busy with breastworks and skirmishing. The contemporary accounts tell how the besieged 'began a breast work from a wall on the south side of the orchard . . .' and 'this day we began blocking up the south port . . . and lining the houses on each side . . .', while the besiegers equally energetically 'began to entrench between Barton Street and the Friars Barn' and 'made a kind of mine to drain the moat, which much sink the water'.

Numerous small attacks were made by both sides, typical descriptions being 'the enemy attempted to make a passage over the moat . . . but being descried by our sentinels, they were beaton off with some loss by our muskettiers', and of two parties who 'sallied out for the nailing of the enemy's cannon'. 200 musketeers sallied forth from the north gate under Captain Moore, but the guide 'foolishly mistaking the way brought them round to Sir Jacob Astley's quarters at the Barton. Despite this error, which might have cost them dear, they were brought off safeley.'

Dorney explains: 'The safety of the whole did require these frequent sallies, a desperate remedy to a despairing city; not only to cast back the enemy's preparations, but to amaze them, that the soldiers should be held up in such hight of resolution, and cause them to expect more hot service from within the works.' Obviously a psychological as well as physical deterrent to storming. The Royalists had now placed three batteries 'one at Gawdy Green as afore said, and now three more [cannon] on the east side of the Friars orchard neare Rignall stile within lesse than pistoll shott of the town-wall and two more in another battery neare the east gate'. With a limited supply of powder the Roundheads were compelled to use their ordnance only when necessary, but there was apparently no shortage on the Royalists' side, the siege accounts being full of reports such as 'most furious battery . . . one hundred and fifty great shot . . . shrewdly battering the wall', and so on.

While all casualty lists and reports of damage must be regarded with suspicion, there seems little doubt that the besiegers intended to beat the 'unfortunate and obstinate town'[10] to pieces about the citizens' ears and march in over the ruins. On 24 August, a surrender demand to 'perswade the yeelding up of the citie in regard of the great power and terrible threats of the enemy, and small hopes, and in a manner impossibilitie of relief . . .' was made. To this speech the garrison returned 'a resolute negative answer and so [they] departed'. At this the disappointed Royalists replied with a heavy bombardment: 'in the afternoon their ordnance played from Gawdie Green, and they likewise from thence shot many grenadoes . . . they shot . . . great fire balls [and] great stones out of their morter pieces.'

In the evening and night, the Llanthoney battery joined in firing 'about twenty fiery melting hot iron bullets, some eighteen pound, others twenty two pound weight, in the night wee perceived them flying in the ayre like a star shooting'. The defenders seem to have been on the alert for these incendiary devices, for although a number fell into haylofts and houses they were all extinguished. One fell into the room of the local apothecary, but someone 'cast many payles of water upon it to quench the same, but the little avayling it was cast into a cowle of water, where after a good space it cooled'. To combat a rumour that the town had fallen, three lights were set up on the College tower to 'give notice of our holding out'. Fodder for the horses now began to be short so the garrison mounted a series of hay raids 'and fetched it from Walham'. The enemy naturally enough sent a party out to fire the cocks, 'which some by reason of our shot, I believe, dearely repented'.

Mining and counter-mining were now proceeding. Both sides had trouble with the underground springs. The dangers of the miners in their dark, narrow and airless tunnels are graphically described by Corbet: 'at length our miners could heare them work under them, and did expect to spoil them by pouring in water or stealing out their powder'. That the nursery rhyme 'Humpty Dumpty' had a very solid factual background is shown: 'We understood likewise that the enemy had . . . provided great store of engines after the manner of the *Romane Testudinas cum Pluteis* with which they intended to have assaulted the parts of the citie.' Apparently they ran on cart wheels with a 'blinde of plankes musquet proofe and holes forefoure mousqueteers to play out off . . . and carrying a bridge before it. The wheeles were to fall into our ditch and the end of the bridge to rest upon our brest workes . . . to enter the city.' After the siege these engines were brought into the city and doubtless dismembered and 'all the kings horses and all the kings men couldn't put Humpty Dumpty together again'.

Message arrows were now sent into the town 'the contents of which as follows: . . . "Your God Waller has forsaken you and Essex is beaten like a dog, yield to the Kings mercie in time . . ."' to which some wag amongst the garrison answered '". . . Be sure ere long ye shall be soundly beaten. Quarter we ask you none, if we fall downe, King Charles will lose true subjects in the towne . . ."' and signed it Nicholas Cudgel-you well. It is not surprising that this spirit and firmness of purpose caused the King himself to 'wonder at our confidence and whence we expected succour, adding . . . Waller is extinct and Essex cannot come,' for after the surrender of Bristol Fiennes himself had been of the opinion that 'they would be hanged if Gloucester could hold out for two days if the enemy came before it'.

But the garrison had hope that relief was on its way and at last this was confirmed when two signal fires were lighted on Waynload Hill by scouts who had been sent out to this vantage point to watch the road, in the direction of London. Perhaps they had been given the use of the perspective glasses (telescopes) which Dorney tells us that the garrison had been using to spy on the enemy positions. Lights were again shown in the college tower in acknowledgement.

September 5 dawned and as many as could be spared from the defences went to church to pray for deliverance. Those on the walls eventually saw laden wagons moving out, the Royalists 'having stayed with us to the last hour, not knowing what a moment might bring forth'.

The garrison was not taking any chances of falling victims of a ruse at this late stage, as Corbet explains: 'This evening the Lord General came to the brow of the hills seven miles from the town and fired a warning piece, but by reason of the contrary winds the report was not heard, neither did the news reach us that night . . . wherefore . . . [we] kept as strong a watchful guard as at any time before'.

However, there could be little doubt that the siege was raised. The King, doubtless did not wish to hazard his cavalry in that broken country, but preferred to await an opportunity to engage Essex at a more suitable venue; which indeed he did, barring the way at Wash Common near Newbury, with negative results. Down to their last three barrels of gunpowder, short of almost every necessity, the joy and relief of the hard-pressed citizens of Gloucester as they heard the staccato challenge of the drums, the triumphant psalm tune, the marching feet approaching and then the sight of the bright banners of the relief force that had saved them at the eleventh hour was fervently summed up by Dorney: 'We therefore perceived that God had delivered us, and we were freed from those that had so long thirsted for our blood. To Him therefore be the honour and glory. Amen.'

REFERENCES

1 Washbourn, *Bibliotheca Gloucestrensis*, Vol. 2, p. lvii (1825 edition). This contains Corbet, *The Military Government of Gloucester*, 1645, and Dorney, *A Brief and Exact Relation of the Siege Laid Before the City of Gloucester*, 1643
2 *Ibid*, Vol. 2, p. 57
3 Corbet, p. 11
4 Dorney, p. 209
5 *Ibid*
6 *Ibid*, p. 210
7 Warburton *Memoirs of Prince Rupert and the Cavaliers*, 1849, Vol. II, p. 281
8 Dorney, 211
9 *Ibid*, 212
10 Clarendon, Vol. VII, p. 298

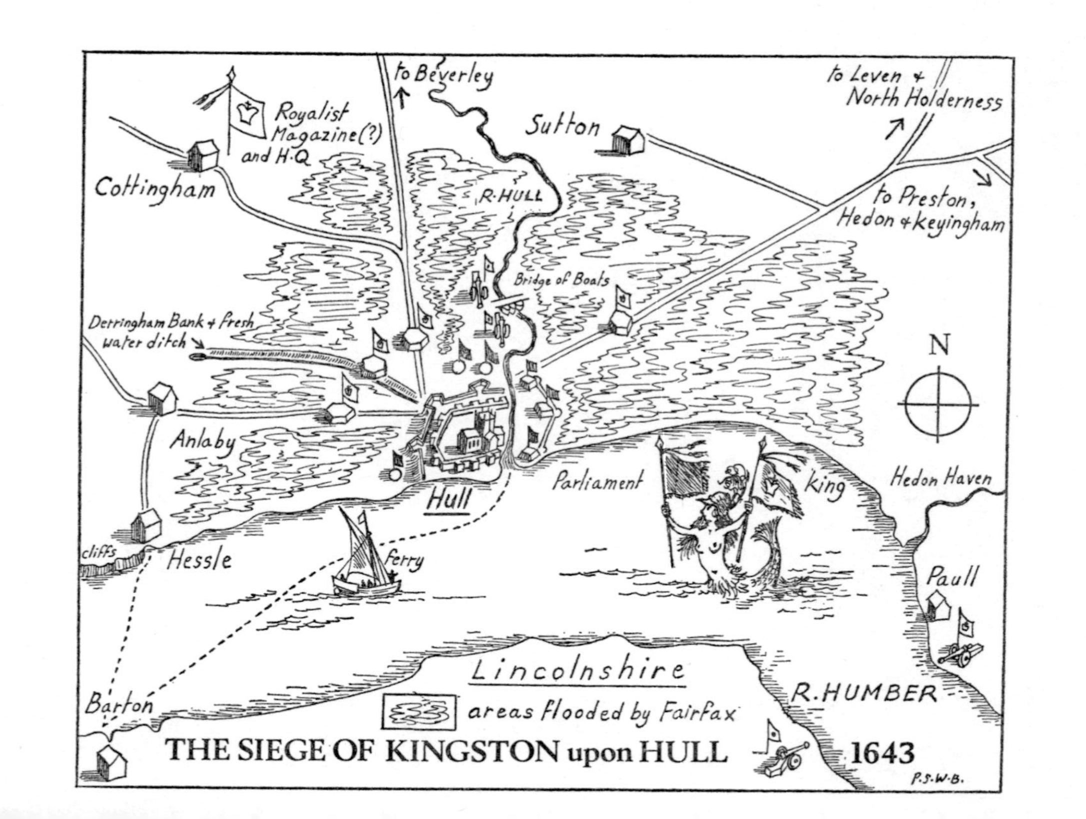
to Beverley
Royalist Magazine(?) and H.Q
Cottingham
Sutton
to Leven & North Holderness
to Preston, Hedon & Keyingham
R. HULL
Bridge of Boats
Derringham Bank & Fresh water ditch
N
Anlaby
Hull
Parliament
King
Hedon Haven
cliffs
Hessle
Ferry
Paull
Lincolnshire
R. HUMBER
Barton
areas flooded by Fairfax
THE SIEGE OF KINGSTON upon HULL
1643
P.S.W.B.

Hull

Defender:	(1) Sir John Hotham (P)
	(2) Ferdinando Lord Fairfax (P)
Besieger:	(1) a. King Charles I
	b. Earl of Newport (R)
	(2) Marquis of Newcastle (R)
Duration:	(1) Most of July 1642
	(2) 2 September–12 October 1643
Outcome:	(1) Siege raised due to lack of materials and men
	(2) Royalists raised siege

Hull, or to give it its full title Kingston-upon-Hull, was, by the fifteenth century, the third most important port in the country, yet less is known of its early history than many comparable cities, not only because of the meagre documentary sources but also because the high water table beneath Hull makes deep excavation difficult and expensive. It was not until the proposed extensive redevelopment of the area made an archaeological investigation almost a necessity that the first trial excavations were made in 1964 and again in 1969.

The findings, allied to the seventeenth century map by Hollar and the view by Buck,[1] have disclosed that the town walls were 4 feet 6 ins thick at their foundations and an estimated height of 14 feet to the parapet walk, and that they were constructed of brick between 1321 and 1400, the first large scale use of that material in this country.[2] The 12 interval towers uncovered by excavation were shown to have been oblong, the internal measurements being 23 feet by 15 feet, their height being computed at 29 feet.

Prior to the building of these walls, it would appear that the defences consisted of a moat connecting the River Hull to the Humber, thus forming a triangle; the excavated material being thrown inward to form a palisaded bank which was retained as a backing to strengthen the walls and towers when they were added.

The four gatehouses shown in Hollars' map (*c.* 1640) appear to be merely interval towers equipped with gates and drawbridges. The southernmost portal was situated by the riverside, giving access to the road to Hessle and hence, not unnaturally, was named the Hessle

Gate; the second, the Myton Gate, opened on to a minor road, while the Beverley Gate (seemingly the main entrance) let on to the Anlaby road. At the further extremity next to the Hull River the North Gate was situated, from which wound the Hedon road across a bridge.

These defences were apparently considered adequate until the reign of Henry VIII, who ordered a line of fortifications to be built along the bank of the River Hull to protect the exposed eastern front of the town and the Old Harbour. John Rogers, a celebrated military engineer, was commissioned to construct them. The scheme was quite simple,[3] consisting of three great blockhouses joined by heavy curtain walls, the whole being about half a mile in length. The fort which was situated where Hull joined Humber was known rather unimaginatively as the South Blockhouse, while similarly its companion at the opposite end – which overlapped the town walls so that it commanded the Hedon Bridge – was the North Blockhouse. Approximately midway between the two the third strongpoint was the somewhat grandiosely named castle. Further excavations in 1970 proved the castle to be rectangular in shape with an internal courtyard and central keep.[4] The brick walls strengthened with limestone quoins on the exposed angles were 19 feet thick, while the subordinate blockhouses were of trefoil design with walls 15 feet thick. The whole line of fortifications was fronted by a moat. From this description it will be seen that Rogers interpreted his royal master's injunction to build it 'mighty strong' quite literally, at a cost of £23000.

Some time before 1642 the main gates of the town were strengthened with earthen bastions, together with a second moat known as the Bush Dyke.

Of all these formidable fortifications which, allied with the natural strength of the position, made the town almost impregnable, nothing now remains above ground, although the last of the Tudor bastions were not demolished until as recently as 1864.

The Sieges

Hull was placed on a war footing sooner than most places dealt with in this book, for it served as the arsenal for the war with Scotland. With the road system hardly more than a network of muddy tracks,[5] it was infinitely faster and more convenient to send stores and equipment by sea, using Hull as a focal point from which they might be issued at need. Armaments bought in Holland to the value of £6000 were stored in the Old Manor House, and issues were made in April 1639 to that part of the army that lay at York, and also to Berwick and Newcastle.

As the country moved towards civil war, a certain amount of jockeying for position took place. Strafford, shrewdly assessing the strategic value of the town, wrote to the Corporation in September 1640, ordering it to quarter Sir Thomas Glemham, appointed as Governor, and his regiment of foot. With the execution of Strafford, Parliament intrigued to get the ardently Royalist Governor removed and replaced by one sympathetic to themselves. In July 1641, this was achieved and Sir Jacob Astley and Captain Will Legge arrived to disband the regiment and restore the Mayor's authority.

In the January of the next year, with war clouds looming on the horizon, Parliament took the opportunity of putting garrisons into the northern ports of Tynemouth, Newcastle and Scarborough, while Sir John Hotham raised the East Yorkshire trained bands and occupied Hull. Naturally this was done covertly, for affairs had not yet come to a head, but when the King left York on 23 April, sending a messenger on ahead to inform Hotham that he would 'dine with him that day', the mask was off.

Hotham, conferring with Peregrine Pelham and other prominent citizens, divining that Charles's real purpose was to seize the magazine and arm his followers, concluded they must take the dangerous decision to deny the King entry. Although a message was sent to that effect, the Royal party still advanced on the town only to discover that the gates were closed and the drawbridges raised. There was nothing the King could do and eventually he was forced to retire to Beverley and on 24 April, somewhat futilely, he sent his heralds and formally declared Hotham a traitor. Although the King's standard had not yet been raised, recruiting in earnest started in June 1642 with the issues of commissions of array, and during the first week in July the Earl of Lindsey, using the Yorkshire trained bands, blockaded the port and built three forts to command the Humber.

Meanwhile, Hotham had not been idle for, realising that war had already started as far as Hull was concerned, he caused the countryside to be swept bare of cattle and sheep within a four-mile radius and brought safely within the walls. A breastwork was constructed round the town from Hessle Gate to North Gate while all the buildings outside the defences were levelled to deny cover to the enemy. When, as a final touch, the low lying terrain to the west was flooded by taking advantage of a high spring tide, the town was as nearly impregnable as the act of man could make it.

The attempt was premature, for in this early stage the Royal Army was ill-equipped for the field, let alone for the specialised business of siege warfare. When Rear Admiral Thomas Trenchfield arrived with several ships of the Parliament Navy carrying 1500 men to supplement the troops of Sir John Meldrum who had already arrived by sea – blasting Lindsey's forts with his ships' ordnance as he passed – the Parliamentarians felt strong enough to launch an attack. Issuing from the Beverley Gate, they attacked the Royalists around Anlaby and drove them from their trenches, setting fire to a barn in which ammunition was stored. Being totally untrained, the King's foot turned and fled. Charles had relinquished the command on 17 July to the Earl of Newport and returned to York. It was upon the latter's order that the besiegers withdrew. All that had really been achieved had been to underline the priceless tactical advantage of sea power in which, unfortunately for Charles, Parliament predominated.

The second siege commenced on 2 September 1643, when Newcastle, having driven the Parliamentarians from Beverley, beleaguered Hull with an army 15000 strong. They commenced operations immediately, working on batteries and entrenchments, diverting the fresh water supply, commandeering all the food stuffs. By 5 September a bridge of boats had been thrown across the Hull north of the town, together with a fort provided with two cannon. To counter this, Fairfax constructed a strongpoint on the site of the Carthusian monastery (The Charterhouse) about a quarter mile outside the town walls. The Royalists' next move was to build yet another fort, named for the King, which, it has been suggested, was sited in the vicinity of the juncture of the modern-day Oxford Street with Wincolmlee. Naturally this position came under heavy fire from both the North Blockhouse and the town walls, although it has been thought to have been screened from Charterhouse by the river bank.

As though the opponents were playing a game of chess. Fairfax countered by building yet another position, 400 yards from Charterhouse whence guns could be brought to bear on the King's Fort, which, by now, was not only supplied with ordnance but also with a furnace for heating shot.

Four days later the garrison made a determined attack with a party of about 400 horse and foot against the Royalists at Anlaby, where, however, they were repelled with such vehemence that they were driven back into the shelter of the town's cannon.

Despite the strength of the Hull defences, Fairfax seems to have desired to make assurance doubly sure, for on 13 September he ordered the sluices to be opened causing the low lying countryside surrounding the town to be flooded, a move that had a double-edged result, for while it flooded the Royalists out of some of their works it also made it practically impossible to obtain fodder for the garrison's horses.

At this time the Parliamentarians were almost undone by the carelessness of one of their own soldiers. With almost inconceivable stupidity, he entered one of the magazines in the North Blockhouse with a naked flame, and predictably the charges stored there blew up! Fortunately, so massive was the construction of the Blockhouse that a large number of barrels of powder stored in adjacent magazines were not affected. Had they exploded, the Blockhouse, the Hedon Bridge and probably the North Gate bastion would have been demolished.

The lethargic Newcastle seems hardly to have exerted himself to harass the enemy and press home the siege, despite his great numbers, for on 20 September Willoughby and Cromwell were able to cross the river and enter the besieged town for a conference, which resulted in Sir Thomas Fairfax being despatched with 25 troops of horse across the Humber into Lincolnshire. Colonel Sir John Henderson, the Governor of Newark, attempted to impede this operation but was not in sufficient strength to prevent it. It might seem that to a general of ordinary talents it would have been obvious that by using a section of his force to occupy Barton, Newcastle could have sealed the garrison off from their friends. On 27 September Newcastle order the fort at Paull and a complementary one at Whitgift on the south bank of Humber to be built in an effort to command the passage of the river, but these were blasted by the Parliament warships before they could be completed.

Three days later, the Royalists suffered a major disaster when their main magazine at Cottingham blew up. Whether this was an accident or whether it was the result of an early commando-type raid, organised by some daring officer who remembered the profitable results of the Anlaby raid during the first siege, is not known.

The crucial day of the siege was 9 October, when without warning a two-pronged attack was made on the defences. Newcastle struck at the Charterhouse fort and Captain Strickland simultaneously attacked the

5

fort near the west jetty. The first attack overran the Charterhouse battery, but before the guns could be spiked, the townsfolk swarmed through the North Gate, counter-attacking so vigorously that the Royalists were driven back with the loss of a captain and a number of soldiers. Similarly, Strickland's attack was initially successful. Taking the fort's garrison by surprise, he was climbing the wall before he was perceived and fired upon by the men manning the Hessle Gate redoubt. Abandoning the fort attack, Strickland charged the redoubt and although the entrance was so narrow that it would admit only two abreast, they reached the top and at the moment that the captain was demanding (somewhat optimistically) their surrender, he was shot by a garrison soldier, who seemingly had different views. With the death of their leader, all the heart went out of the raiders, and they retreated with great loss.

Lord Fairfax, deciding to retaliate in strength, ordered all the garrison 'without beat of drum' on 11 October, and at 9 a.m. a feint attack was made towards the Charterhouse to distract the enemy's attention from the main attack of 1500 men that had been divided into three columns issuing from the three western gates. The first line of Royalist trenches, about half a mile from the town, fell after a fierce resistance, as did the second. At this critical moment the Royalist reserves counter-attacked, driving the garrison back almost to the town walls, where Meldrum and Fairfax reformed and rallied them.

Launching a further attack the Parliamentarians were everywhere successful. Beating the Royalists back, they overran their batteries and, turning the guns, blasted their retreating owners with them. Two great guns named Gog and Magog, were captured, together with a demi culverin, four drakes mounted on a single carriage, two large drakes and a saker.[6]

At dawn the next day the garrison perceived that the Royalists had received such a salutory check that they were abandoning the siege and withdrawing to York, devastating the countryside as they went.

REFERENCES

1. There is also a drawing of the City wall, sectioned with scale, dated 1742, in the Civic Records
2. See Kingston-upon-Hull Museum *Bulletin*, Nos. 3 & 4, 1969 and 1970

[3] Some of Rogers' design plans still exist in the British Museum (Cotton MS. Supps. 4 & 20)

[4] *Bulletin*, No. 6, 1971

[5] See Parkes, *Travel in the Seventeenth Century*, 1968

[6] See Wildridge, *Old and New Hull*, 1884

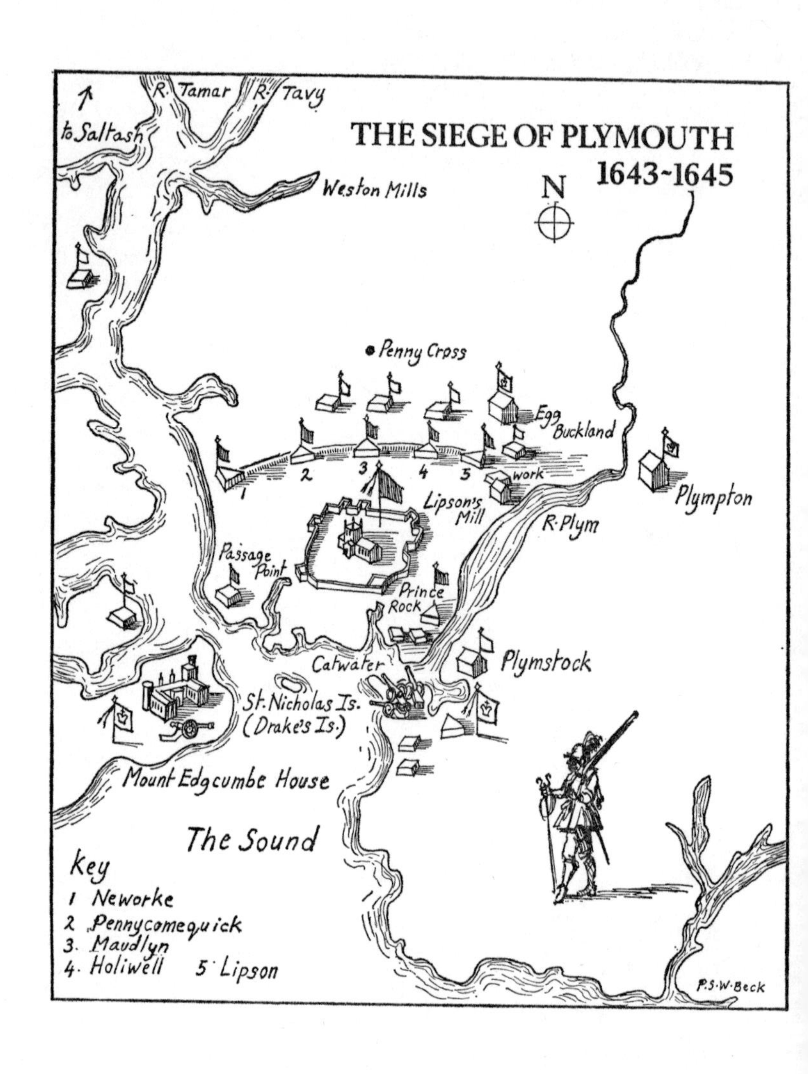
THE SIEGE OF PLYMOUTH
1643~1645
to Saltash
R. Tamar
R. Tavy
Weston Mills
N
Penny Cross
Egg Buckland
work
Plympton
Lipson's Mill
R. Plym
Passage Point
Prince Rock
Plymstock
Catwater
St. Nicholas Is.
(Drake's Is.)
Mount Edgcumbe House
The Sound
Key
1 Neworke
2 Pennycomequick
3. Maudlyn
4. Holiwell
5 Lipson
P.S.W. Beck

Plymouth

Defender: Colonel James Wardlaw (P)
Besieger: Prince Maurice (R)
Duration: 30 September–22 December 1643
Outcome: Royalists abandoned siege

Probably the best-known port, historically, in the land, Plymouth achieved commercial maturity rather later than many others, but was thriving by the thirteenth century. The most famous incident in its annals is, of course, that game of bowls played on Plymouth Hoe by Sir Francis Drake, who maintained that he had ample time to finish the game *and* trounce the Armada. Doubtless, having a mind to the state of wind and tide, he made the remark as a morale booster. Not perhaps so well known is the fact that the port supplied many ships during the Hundred Years' War against the French, and that from here Hawkins, Raleigh and Frobisher embarked on their great voyages.

From here also, when one of their ships, the *Speedwell*, sprang a leak, causing them to put into Plymouth for repairs, the Pilgrim Fathers set out to found a new nation in 1620. The house where they are supposed to have gathered for the last time on English soil and the Mayflower steps from which they embarked are still in existence. From here also in 1772 Captain James Cook R.N. departed on his three-year circumnavigation of the world, emulating Drake who had been the first Englishman to do so.

With such a wealth of tradition, it is not surprising that the citizens became a special breed, independent and self-assertive, who, despite their internal quarrels and differences, presented a united front to an enemy, giving rise to the proud boast that in all Devonshire, Plymouth was the only community that did not change hands during the Civil War, but adhered firmly to its Parliamentary principles.

The Sieges

The army that Sir Ralph Hopton had raised for the King in loyal Cornwall in 1642 was everywhere successful, although a ludicrous incident had occurred when he initially arrived in the county, and was arraigned at Truro assizes for bringing armed forces into the Duchy! Realising that he would have difficulty in persuading the trained bands to cross the Tamar, he and the other Cavalier-orientated landowners recruited an army of five full-strength regiments, all volunteers, and more than 500 horse.

Startled by this intelligence, Parliament as a counter-measure ordered the Deputy Lieutenant of Cornwall to raise 1000 men and instructed two troops of horse to attach themselves to this body. Later in October, it also commanded the Committee of Devon to provide 500 dragoons and sent the Earl of Bedford westward with seven more troops of horse and 1000 men.

But still Hopton raided across the Tamar and in December cut off Plymouth's water supply. The Committee, now thoroughly alarmed for the town's safety, gave Lord John Robartes the command and ordered that three regiments of volunteers and 1000 dragoons should be raised for the town's defence.

The first attempt to close in on Plymouth was doomed to failure because of insufficient numbers. The Royalists seized Mount Edgecumbe House and Millbrook and secured the Cornish side of the Sound, but that was all they could do. So Hopton, to implement his numbers, invoked the ancient *Posse Comitatus*, but the Devonians were totally disinclined to such warlike proceedings and when they turned out, as they were legally obliged to do, on 6 December at Modbury, they were, as Hopton disgustedly remarked, 'rather like a great fair than a posse'.

Here the Roundheads took a hand in the game, for, under General Ruthin, they attacked the gathering by night, dispersing the posse which fled in all directions, capturing the High Sheriff and other Devonshire gentlemen, while Hopton and Sir Nicholas Slanning escaped only by the narrowest of narrow margins.

This abortive attempt to siege Plymouth was succeeded by a head-on confrontation, at the battle of Braddock Down, on 19 January 1643, when after a three-hour fight Ruthin's forces were driven pell-mell from the field and Hopton was undisputed master of Cornwall.

On 22 January 1643, the Royalists re-invaded Devon. Hopton and Lord Mohun stormed Saltash, capturing 140 prisoners, four guns and a ship of 400 tons, mounting 16 cannon. Still labouring under the handicap of Cornish trained bands who refused to leave their county, Hopton had to be content to blockade Plymouth, for without them he just had not sufficient numbers for a regular siege.

With a display of the aggressive spirit already alluded to, a Roundhead force, under James Chudleigh, fell upon Modbury at 1 p.m. on 21 February. The Royalists resisted fiercely, the action continuing through the evening and into the night. Eventually they broke, leaving 100 dead, 150 prisoners, 1100 muskets and five guns.

Next morning, Hopton's army once again retired across the River Tamar, falling back on Tavistock. The rest of the year 1643 was occupied with field actions; Launceston 23 April, Sourton Down 25 April, Stratton 16 May, the last being Hopton's greatest victory from which, when ennobled, he was to take his title.

He was at Launceston when he knew for certain that Maurice and Hertford were marching to join him at Chard, so thither he went, leaving forces to blockade both Exeter and Plymouth. From there the trio moved out of the scope of this narrative at least for the time being, engaging in several successful field actions terminating with the storm of Bristol.

After these important victories, the Western Army, under Maurice, was ordered to return and reduce Exeter and Plymouth, thus completing the conquest of Devon. Exeter surrendered on 4 September 1643 following Barnstable's example two days previously, so that when Dartmouth fell on 5 October, Plymouth was in the lion's mouth.

On 30 September Colonel James Wardlaw with 500 men arrived in Plymouth, replacing the Mayor as military Governor, and making it quite plain that there would be no surrender just so long as one brick stood on another and there was one man left alive.[1]

The Royalist commander, Colonel John Digby, had maintained a mild blockade since the previous August, which the garrison had either accepted or ignored. With the advent of Wardlaw there was a change of attitude. Parliamentary sallies became the order of the day, that is, until the arrival of Maurice with nine regiments of foot and five of horse, which were stationed in an arc stretching from Plymstock in the east to Mount Edgecumbe in the west, via Plympton, Egg Buckland, Tamerton and Saltash.[2] Within two weeks Mount Stamford was captured and batteries set up which bombarded the town across the narrow Catwater.

The longstanding arguments between the authorities and the military of the town, aggravated by this bombardment, flared up again. Some wished to negotiate a settlement, others disapproved of the way the defence was conducted and others wished to fight to the death.[3] All learned what it was to be under martial law. Wardlaw made them understand that his was the only voice, and reiterated that he would incinerate the town and all in it before he surrendered, and demanded of all citizens that they took an oath to 'faithfully maintain and defend' the town.[4] On 16 November the besiegers assaulted the northern works, as a psychological prelude to sending a summons guaranteeing a full pardon for all within if they would surrender.[5] Not unnaturally this offer met with a stony silence.

Ellis Carteret, Henry Pike and Moses Collins, Royalist supporters, tried to bribe the garrison of the Maudlyn Fort into blowing up its magazine,[6] but the stout-hearted captain arrested Carteret and almost secured Pike and Collins, who escaped to the Royalist lines, returning that evening with 400 musketeers whom they had promised to lead through the Roundhead defences. At daybreak on 3 December, they surprised the guard at Laira Point and took Lipton's from the rear, but even so, were unable to gain it. A force of 450 horse and foot of the garrison rushed out and engaged them. Both sides being reinforced, a skirmish developed, lasting for some hours until the Royalists retired, their retreat being hindered by the rising tide and the fire of a Roundhead warship.[7]

On 18 December, the Royalists concentrated a heavy bombardment on the Maudlyn Fort, the key to the outer defences, which continued for two days. An entrenchment that had been constructed by the besiegers to cut off relief from Pennycomequick was assaulted and destroyed by the garrison after two desperate charges.[8]

The Royalist council of war apparently concluded that they were wasting their time and the town could not be taken. On 22 December they started a withdrawal which was completed on Christmas Day, although a blockade remained. Maurice moved his army into winter quarters and issed a warrant to the surrounding districts threatening severe penalties to anyone aiding Plymouth with food or other goods.[9] In their stout defence and in their defiance of the later blockade, the citizens served the Parliamentary cause better than they knew, causing the King to use men and material to maintain their isolation that would have been useful elsewhere.

REFERENCES

1 Clarendon, Vol. V, p. 297
2 *A True Narration of the Most Observable passages* . . . , Seymour Papers;

Devon County Record Office, No. 1392; See also *A Letter from Plymouth* . . . , British Museum, Thomason Tracts, E74 (22) 1–3

3 *The Copy of a letter sent from the Commander in Chief*, British Museum, Thomason Tracts, E76 (11)

4 *A True Narration* . . .

5 *Ibid*

6 Rushworth, *Historical Collections*, 1721–2

7 *Weekly Account*, British Museum, Thomason Tracts E.78 (29) 3

8 *A True Narration* . . . states the besiegers lost 100 killed and the attackers about the same number killed and wounded

9 *A True Narration* . . .

Lathom House

Defender:	(1) Charlotte, Countess of Derby (R) (2) Colonel Edward Rosthern (R) (Rawstern, Rosethorn)
Besieger:	(1) Sir Thomas Fairfax (P) (2) Major General Egerton (P)
Duration:	(1) 28 February–27 May 1644 (2) July 1644–2 December 1645
Outcome:	(1) Relieved by Prince Rupert (2) Surrendered on terms

The mighty pile of Lathom House (near Ormskirk) and the Italianate mansion that succeeded it are no more. All that remains of either are a block of buildings, once the stables and coach-house of the latter. Excavations in the nineteenth century seem to suggest that the older house was sited somewhat to the east of these and to have been built of red sandstone. The Earl of Derby's chaplain at the time of the Civil War (the Reverend S. Rutter, later Bishop of Sodor and Man) has compared the situation of the house to the 'palm of a man's hand, flat in the middle, and covered with a rising round about it, and so near to it, that the enemy during the siege, were never able to raise a battery against it, so as to make a breach in the wall, practicable to enter the house by way of storm'.[1] Apparently it was surrounded by a 'strong wall two yards thick, there were nine towers on the wall, flanking each other, with six guns in each, three facing in each direction', and the gate-house comprised 'two high and strong buildings, with a strong tower on each side of it'.

Beside these defences there was 'a high, strong tower called the Eagle Tower in the midst of the house, surmounting all the rest', while 'without the wall was a moat eight yards wide, and two deep; upon the back of the moat, between the wall and the graff, was a strong row of palisades around'.

The first Earl of Derby is said to have considerably enlarged and improved Lathom House in 1496 for a visit by Henry VII; seemingly the residence was of some antiquity even then. At the end of the second siege when the house was obliged to surrender 'the soldiers with wild ferocity . . . turned what had been a place of beauty and splendour into a scene of destruction, spoliation and ruin'.

The Siege

With some truth, Roby in *Tradition of Lancashire* asserts that 'Lord Derby . . . had been commanded to leave the realm and proceed to the Isle of Man, at the precise time when his presence here would have been the most serviceable', for on 28 February 1644 Captain Markland brought a letter from Sir Thomas Fairfax requiring the Countess to[2] 'yield up Lathom House upon such honourable conditions as he should propose'. To this the Lady replied that 'she wondered that Sir Thomas Fairfax should require her to give up her lord's house, without any offence . . . to Parliament', and asked for a week to consider his proposals 'both to resolve the doubts of conscience and to advise in matters of law and honour'.

The Parliament Army investing the house consisted of some 2500 men under four colonels, Ralph Ashton, – Holland, John Moore and Alexander Rigby.[3] Messages went back and forth until 12 March, the Countess (who belonged to the warlike French family of La Trémouille) playing for time, arguing with regard to the venue for the meeting 'conceiving it must be more knightly that Sir Thomas Fairfax should wait on her rather than she on him'.

Well might she procrastinate for her resources were of the most slender. She had not a single officer of field rank. Her six captains were William Farmer (killed at Marston Moor), William (?) Farrington of Werden, – Charnock of Charnock, Edward Chisenhall of Chisenhall, Edward Rosthern (Rosethorne, Rawstern) of New Hall, Henry Ogle of Prescot, Richard Fox and Molyneux Radcliff.[4]

Lieutenant William Key commanded 12 horse and there were 300 foot organised into six companies, each 50 strong. The ordnance (despite the chaplain's description) consisted of six sakers ($5\frac{1}{4}$ pounders) and two sling pieces. The towers – accounts vary whether there were seven or nine – were manned during the hours of daylight by picked marksmen and also contained one or two 'murderers' for scouring the ditches.

The Roundheads had not been idle during this waiting period, but had circumvallated the house. 'Their works were an open trench round the house, a yard of ditch, and a yard of raised with turf at the distance of sixty, one hundred or two hundred yards from the walls.'

Eight sconces were raised at strategic points, constructed 'with two yards of rampart and a yard of ditch, in some places staked and palisaded to keep off a violent assault'.[5] To construct these, they had used the usual methods of protection for their pioneers described in the first chapter.

Farmer led the first sortie,[6] 'determined to do something that might remind the enemy that there were soldiers within'. He marched up to their works without a shot, and then firing upon them in their trenches they quickly left their holes. The horse, issuing out from another gate, attacked the fleeing Roundheads stoutly, with some slaughter.

The Roundhead ordnance, consisting of a demi-cannon (24 pounder) and a culverin (15 pounder), three sakers ($5\frac{1}{4}$ pounders) and a mortar, opened fire on 20 March. The siege journal from which these quotations are taken comments:[7] 'They first tried the wall, [with the demi-cannon] which being found proof, without yielding or showing the least impression; they afterwards shot higher to beat down the pinnacles and turrets or else to please the women that came to see the spectacle.'

On 25 March the bombardment was intensified, the 24 pounder being augmented by the culverin, while three days later all five of the cannon opened fire. On 10 April 'during the day and night, [they] loaded with chain shot and bars of iron were shot against the house'. Deadly though the peril was from these missiles, one of which 'struck the battlements upon one of our marksmen . . . and crushed him to death,' it was the mortar that really disheartened the garrison. On the next day this weapon, 13 inches in diameter, that Rigby had borrowed from Sir William Brereton,[8] hurled three stone each weighing 80 pounds on the target.

The fiery Farmer seems to have felt that they had sat too long under this hail of missiles without retaliation, for taking half the garrison and seconded by Lieutenants Penketh and Worrill he beat the Roundheads from their works, took 60 sets of arms and attempted to spike the guns, and calmly marched back through the main gates. There was a novel innovation, for 'Captain Fox by a colour from the Eagle Tower gave signal when to march and when to retreat, according to the motions of the enemy'.[9]

Despite the steel nails the Royalists had driven in the touch holes to silence the guns, they were not silent for long. On 15 April, the mortar again fired five times with stones and once with a granado. Five days later 30 shots from the two heavy guns were poured into a postern tower. On Easter Monday (22 April) the bombardment was stepped up, presumably for propaganda purposes, for it being a holiday, a crowd of country folk had turned out to witness the spectacle.

Imagining by now that the garrison would have had enough, Rigby sent a surrender notice by a drummer. But he had reckoned without the lady's fighting spirit. Tearing the demand into fragments, she told the drummer grimly, 'A due reward for thy pains would be to hang thee at my gate, but thou art only the foolish instrument of a traitor's pride. Take this answer back to Rigby . . .', and no doubt playing to the gallery in her turn, she delivered a brief but vehement harangue, saying that sooner than surrender, she and her children would perish in the flames of Lathom House. This fighting speech had its desired effect on the listening soldiers: 'We will die for his Majesty and your honour,' they shouted, 'God save the King!' At a council of war held immediately after the departure of the messenger, it was agreed that the mortar was the great morale breaker and must be neutralised.

It was also agreed that, despite the batteries now covering every exit, they would issue out next morning 'and venture all'. The dispositions were to be as follows: Captain Edward Chisenhall and Captain Richard Fox should lead the sortie; Captain Henry Ogle the main guard, to secure their retreat through the south gate; Captain Rosthern; sally gate on east side to secure retreat; Captain Radcliff, marksmen on the wall; Captain Farmer, reserve on the parade, ready to reinforce any of the parties at need.

At the appointed time, Chisenhall with eight men sallied out of the east gate into the fort where the Roundheads had sited their great guns. After a brisk skirmish, the besiegers fled leaving their dead and wounded behind. Fox now supported Chisenhall and made for the south-eastern corner where the mortar was, beating up the trenches as they went. Their daring was rewarded, for lifting the dread weapon bodily on to a rough sledge they carried it back to the house in triumph. It seems rather amazing that the besiegers never seemed to develop an answer to these lightning raids and to have always been demoralised by such blitzkrieg tactics.

On 23 May the Countess was again summoned to surrender and to submit to the mercy of Parliament. 'The mercies of the wicked are cruel' was her comment.[10] Once more she had struck the right note – once more she was acclaimed by the garrison. But the ordeal was almost over, for that same night a messenger slipped into the house with the glad tidings that Prince Rupert and her husband, having stormed Bolton, were marching to her relief. On the night of 25 May

Rigby, like the Arab, folded his tents and stole away. On 29 May, Sir Richard Crane, commander of the Prince's Lifeguard entered Lathom in triumph to the plaudits of the garrison and presented the Countess with colours captured in the Royalists' latest victory as a tribute to her valour.[11]

The second siege saw Lathom House defended by many of the same officers that took part in the first. The Countess had gone to the Isle of Man with her husband and Edward Rosthern was now Governor of the House, with the rank of Colonel. Under him was Major Munday[12], Captain William Key (Kay), Captains Charnock, Farringdon, Radcliffe, Noel, Worrel, Roby, Tempest and the Reverend S. Rutter, the Chaplain.

High rank had not diminished Rosthern's dash and fire by one iota. Hearing of the approach of the Parliamentary General Egerton with an army of 4000 men, Rosthern ordered out 'a strong body of horse and foot', the latter under Radcliffe and the former under Munday with which he surprised the enemy camp, capturing their whole arsenal of powder and almost capturing the Roundhead General who had perforce to 'fly away in his shirt and slippers'. It has been remarked that 'such were the daring and spirited sallies' that the Parliamentarians who had their headquarters at Ormskirk 'were just as much besieged by the Royalists as the Royalists were by the Parliament at Lathom House'.

But the shadows were lengthening for the supporters of Charles; in fact, Naseby had been fought and lost before the second siege had started. All through that long summer the dreary list of defeats lengthened. Fairfax took Leicester, Fairfax defeated Goring, Bristol surrendered to Fairfax: the Royalists were being defeated everywhere. But still the wild cat sorties went on from Lathom – but it was a war of attrition. Rosthern lost men he could not replace, valuable men like Molyneux Radcliffe. Soon there were shortages of material. The Chaplain, the Reverend Rutter, tells[13] of the many stratagems resorted to to obtain food. The local Royalists smuggled in messages stating that when a fire was lit on the high ground there would be provisions left at that spot. A storming party would then steal out of the house and return laden with corn and bread. If intercepted, they cut their way back into the house. The food thus obtained was 'distributed and divided in the most equal manner . . . three quarters of a pound was weighed to each man alike; the horses that were killed in the service they broiled upon coals . . . frequently without bread or salt'.

When the moat was fouled by the besiegers they dug down and not only found sweet spring water 'but coals as well in great abundance'. With the King at Chester they had great hopes of a relief, but the defeat at Rowton Heath made this impossible. Eventually, on 2 December 1645, Rosthern was compelled to sue for terms and had to be content 'with bare terms of mercy'.

The fall of Lathom House as with Basing was the occasion for the proclamation of a day of thanksgiving at Westminster,[14] and, like Basing, the house, 'once the pride and glory of Lancashire', was razed to the ground.

REFERENCES

1. Bishop Rutter's account is published in Seacombe's *Historical Account of the House of Stanley*
2. *Siege of Lathom House*, printed at the end of *Life of Colonel Hutchinson*, 1846, p. 495
3. *Ibid*, p. 516
4. *Ibid*, p. 515
5. *Siege of Lathom House*, p. 516
6. *Ibid*, p. 500
7. *Ibid*, p. 501
8. C.S.P., p. 129
9. *Siege of Lathom House*, p. 505
10. *Ibid*, p. 512
11. *Ibid*, p. 514
12. *Memoirs of James, Earl of Derby*, p. 157
13. Seacombe
14. *Perfect Diurnal*, 8 December 1645

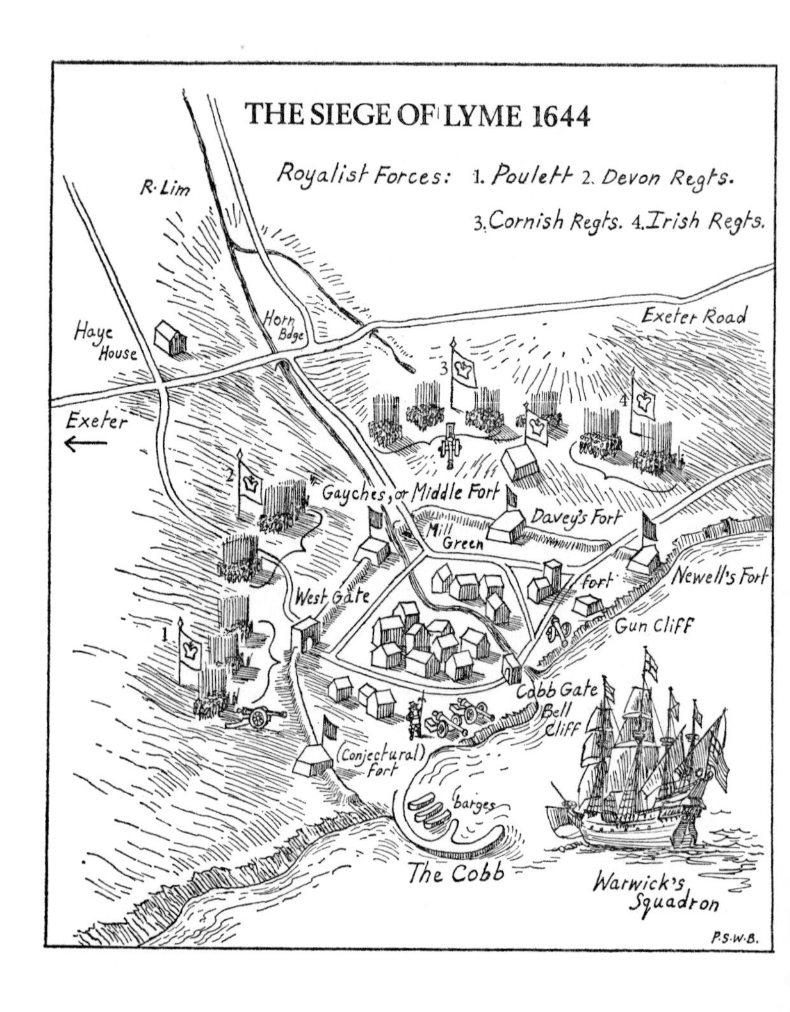
THE SIEGE OF LYME 1644
Royalist Forces: 1. Poulett 2. Devon Regts.
3. Cornish Regts. 4. Irish Regts.
R·Lim
Haye House
Horn Bdge
Exeter Road
Exeter
Gayches, or Middle Fort
Davey's Fort
Mill Green
West Gate
fort
Newell's Fort
Gun Cliff
Cobb Gate
Bell Cliff
(Conjectural) Fort
barges
The Cobb
Warwick's Squadron
P.S.W.B.

Lyme

Defenders:	Garrison Commander: Colonel John Were (P)
	Governor: Colonel – Ceeley (Mayor) (P)
Besieger:	Prince Maurice (R)
Duration:	20 April–15 June 1644
Outcome:	Siege abandoned upon approach of relief force

In the shifting fortunes of war, often the most unlikely places or buildings assume a strategic significance utterly at variance with their customary status.

So it was with Lyme, 'that little vile fishing town' as the besiegers later vexedly described it. Its possession was of triple-fold importance to the Royalists because (a) it would deny an operating base to the Parliament controlled navy and (b) it would terminate the raids that the garrison made, often in concert with the garrison of Poole, upon the loyal heart of the West Country, and, lastly, (c) it was the missing link in a chain of strongholds that would connect the Bristol and English Channels. To anyone familiar with its situation, surrounded by steep hills on three sides, the weakness of its military position is apparent. It had not even the benefit of mediæval walls which might be strengthened for its defence. Some flimsy turf blockhouses and earthworks, hastily constructed to form a defensive ring around the town, was all that there was.[1] As no traces of these earthworks remain (the only surviving relics of the siege being a number of musket and cannon shot in the museum) it is difficult even to conjecture where they were sited in relation to the modern town, but an attempt has been made to locate the blockhouses, and it seems reasonable to suppose that the line of earthworks or even perhaps barricades went the shortest way between each.

It has been conjectured that they described an ellipse commencing on the east at Newell's Fort which commanded the old road to Charmouth. Both road and fort have long since disappeared into the sea owing to coastal erosion.

Davey's Fort is judged to have been on the East Cliff. Westward, over what was doubtless meadowland at that time, the line crossed the River Lim at Mill Green. Hereabouts was Gayches' or the Middle Fort, commanding both the principal road from the town (which led to Horn Bridge where it joined the main Exeter road at right angles) and the river. Bending southward the next strong point was the Western or Marsh's Fort which according to Drake 'serveth[2] well for the securing of the lane going into town', conceivably the juncture of the modern Silver Street and Woodmead Road, from where it swooped down to the sea to another fort near Cobb Gate.

Seaward batteries on Gun Cliff and Bell Cliff commanded the mouth of the River Lim while another, strategically placed, commanded the entrance to the harbour formed by the curving mole called the Cobb which is a feature of Lyme to this day. It is probable that these were provided with demi-culverins (9 pounders) and sakers (5 pounders) which had an excellent field of fire. On the landward side only Davey's and Gayches' could claim to have even a reasonable field of fire and it is clear that if either of them were taken the town was lost.

The Royalist Army made their first appearance late on the afternoon of 20 April 1644, approaching the town in a long column apparently to impress the garrison with their strength, but they 'were not a jot dismayed at the sight . . . but longed to have dealt with them, and so shouted to the enemy, and the enemy answered with shoutings'.

Maurice's army, estimated at 6000 men composed of a motley collection of English, Cornish and Irish troops, caused the prudent Were, no doubt advised and aided by Lieutenant Colonel Robert Blake (later to become one of England's greatest admirals) to withdraw his outposts at Haye and Colway Houses which later became 'very offensive' to the town as strong points.

The action commenced early on the morning of 21 April when the Royalists advanced, apparently bent on taking some cottages close to the defences. To forestall this, the dwellings were fired, but the burning thatch created a thick smoke screen under which the attackers advanced 'brandishing their swords and very boldly shooting at us from the ditches'. A blast of musketry from the defences seems to have cooled their ardour, inflicting some 40 casualties.

Maurice disposed his forces in a horseshoe fashion round the town. The Irish regiments on the east, the four Cornish regiments to the north, with Lord Poulett and the Devon troops to the west. Stedcombe House, which was held by a part of Were's regiment, was taken after fierce fighting occupying 24 hours, the bulk of the defenders cutting their way out and joining the Lyme garrison. Now masters of the locality, the besiegers set about constructing a battery on the western side of the town in which they mounted culverins (27 pounders) and demi-culverins.

On the following morning, Were picked 190 men 'who longed to fight with the enemy more than for a good breakfast',[3] sallied forth at 6 a.m., drove the surprised Royalists from their guns and chased them with slaughter right up the hill until repelled by the main body.

This was only an example of the many raids launched by the garrison against an enemy that outnumbered them five to one. By 25 April another battery appeared opposite the West Gate which compelled the defenders to increase the strength of the fort to 12 feet thick with earth and stones. This was followed by the creation of another battery opposite Davey's Fort which was hastily strengthened by another eight feet, being considered 'the stay of all'.

On Sunday 28 April a major assault was launched by Maurice, which was driven back with great loss as the guns of the town raked the ranks of the stormers with case shot at close range. In vain did the horse endeavour to coerce the foot to return to the charge, even threatening them with the sword, but the sight of 60 to 80 of their comrades lying dead was more than sufficient to discourage them.[4]

Thereafter such a cannonade was maintained by the Royalist gunners that 'their firing seemed[5] a continual blaze'. In fact it was heard out at sea by the Parliament ships, the *Mary Rose* (Captain Somester) and the *Ann and Joyce* (Captain Joyce) which were carrying supplies which included beef, pork, beer, cheese and much[6] needed powder, match, ball and reinforcements. The safe arrival of these vessels 'begat new life in the almost tired soldiers' and must have, however unconsciously, laid the seeds of his future career in Blake's mind, for had not Parliament held command of the sea, the town would have been doomed.[7]

Thus strengthened by the addition of 'the bold seamen', they again issued out against the battery 'lying within a pistol shot of the Western Fort', spiked another gun and inflicted losses so severe 'that the water which served the town was turned to blood'. As with most casualty reports of the period, this must however be taken with reserve.

On 1 May, the Royalists commenced building the Fort Royal opposite to Davey's Fort, no doubt appreciating rather tardily its importance to the defence.

On 5 May, following four days of storm, a sloop was sent to Poole with a letter for the Committee of Both Kingdoms requesting that aid from the land should be sent.

Next day a thick sea fog enveloped the town and the garrison stood to their arms all day in anticipation of an attack. As none materialised, the men stood down about 7 p.m. for supper. Maurice had obviously anticipated this turn of events and now launched a strong attack on three positions, calculating that the sentries would panic and run at the appearance of the Royalists. In this he was mistaken, for the spirit of the Lyme men did not fail them. 'Come on, you rogues, we are ready to receive you',[8] they called and opened a brisk fire, which brought the garrison back at a run. After an hour's hard fighting the attackers were repulsed with a loss of 80 men.

The advantage of sea power was made even more manifest on 8 May, when the ship-of-war *Mayflower* (Captain Cocke) came in with further supplies and on 11 May, a squadron of six ships bearing 300 men from Sir William Waller under the protection of the *Expedition* (Captain Jordan) came in without harm under heavy bombardment from the guns of the furious besiegers.[9]

The *Ann and Joyce* sailed the next day with despatches for Waller and the Committee of Both Kingdoms while the reinforcements were used to increase the small probing attacks which were designed to keep the enemy on their toes. Sometimes these met with more opposition than they cared for, as when a party 'sent to rouse and quicken them on the east quarter of the town . . . but when they were roused, they found them stronger than was thought . . . and retreated without more doing'.[10]

The besiegers determined to stop these supplies coming in from the sea which were negating all their efforts: accordingly they made emplacements for three big guns which they moved from Colway to Holme Bush Fields under cover of darkness on the night of 14 May. Once in place, they were in a position to command the Cobb Gate. The garrison were also mounting two guns loaned by the captains of the *Mary Rose* and *Mayflower*, the one a culverin and the other a demi-culverin.

The following day, the town rocked to the continuous cannonade of 16 guns which directed their fire against the shipping within the Cobb. That the surprise was complete was obvious, for Were comments, 'the ordnance we thought was drawn off began to speak, which had not spoken in three days'. In order to counter these new dispositions, 120 men assaulted the Fort Royal at dawn on 18 May, took ammunition, baggage and 20 prisoners and retired back whence they came.

On 21 May disaster struck the town. Still determined to stop the seaborne supplies, Maurice directed an attack upon the supply barges moored within the Cobb. 60 men charged down on the quay itself, throwing wild fire into the craft, setting fire to 20 of them. The garrison, driven to desperation as they saw the flames shooting skyward, fiercely counter-attacked and drove the musketeers from the new battery but Maurice's horse charged and drove them back, re-entered the Cobb again and resumed the destruction.

Lyme's position was now critical; at one stroke Maurice had almost destroyed their ability to resist. Fortunately, on 23 May a squadron of seven ships was sighted. It was commanded by the Earl of Warwick, Lord High Admiral of England, in his flagship the *James* (48 guns)[11] and consisted of the *Dreadnought* (30), *Expedition* (14), *Warwick**, *Greyhound* (12), *Hind**, and *Seaflower.**

Lieutenant Colonel Robert Blake,[12] with other leaders, rowed out to confer with Warwick, as a result of which 36 barrels of powder, with match proportionate, were landed.

In order to draw the enemy off and give the garrison a respite, Warwick agreed to sail towards Charmouth as though to land troops in Maurice's rear. The feint succeeded, but, when discovered, precipitated another fierce attack, preceded by a heavy bombardment. The defences near the Western Fort were breached and 1000 attackers swarmed to carry the breach. For the first time the defenders showed signs of wavering, but an Ensign, one Edward Moizier, stood in the breach, stoutly waving his colours and his example so heartened the soldiers that they rallied to him. Three times the Royalists returned to the assault 'with as much courage and resolution as could be' only to be driven back to their works with the loss, according to Warwick, of 400 men.

Next, a rather archaic, but effective, device was used.[13] Fire arrows were shot into the town; soon 20 houses were aflame and if it had not been that the breeze was blowing away from the town the tinder-dry thatch which roofed most of the houses would have caught and the town been destroyed. On 30 May the Committee for Both Kingdoms wrote to Waller regarding succour for Lyme: 'Considering that the safety of the Western forts is committed to your care, and many of your forces designed to that end',[14] and on 3 June a messenger was sent to the Earl of Essex requiring him to relieve Lyme or cause Waller to do so.

* Possibly armed merchantmen as their name does not appear in Batten's *Survey of the Fleet* in 1642.

But these two generals were fully occupied with watching King Charles at Oxford. It was not until 6 June that they divided their forces at Burford[15] leaving Waller to watch over the King while Essex proceeded into the West Country. During this time, Warwick's squadron was still lying off Lyme, doing its best to supply the town's needs, which were great. On a 'storming day'[16] the garrison 'having in it 1500 soldiers, including seamen use 15 barrels of powder and every day and every night a quarter ton of match, so there are only 5 or 6 days supply left'.

On 12 June Warwick sent ashore 10 barrels of powder and six boat loads of provisions, and again requested assistance to relieve the town, stating bluntly that the enemy were daily approaching nearer and nearer, and that he could spare no more supplies from his ships 'without visible prejudice to the service'.

But the end of the little town's troubles were in sight. On 12 June Essex had reached Blandford, making Maurice's position untenable. During the following days, the besiegers were seen packing up their tents and moving the cannon out. They were speeded on their way by volleys from Davey's Fort where the valiant captain of that name fired at everything that moved. At 2 a.m. on 15 June, some soldiers fired on the besiegers' works. There was no reply. The siege of Lyme was over: it had cost the Royalists (according to Warwick) 2000 men and the town only six score.

REFERENCES

1 See Article in *The Mariners Mirror*, Vol. 20, October 1934

2 See *The Diary of Edward Drake*, printed in Bayley, *Civil War in Dorset, 1642–1660*, 1910

3 *The Diurnal of Colonel Were*, British Museum, Thomason Tracts, E.51.9

4 *Drake* 5 *Were* 6 *Ibid* 7 *Ibid*

8 *Drake* 9 *Were* 10 *Drake* 11 C.S.P.D. D-IV 544

12 Warwick's letter 10 June 1644; B.M. Thomason Tracts, E.50.23

13 Vicars, *Gods Arke* (Parliamentarie Chronicles), p. 247

14 C.S.P.D. 1644, p. 181

15 For the full circumstances of this division and the subsequent battle see Toynbee and Young, *Cropredy Bridge*, 1970

16 C.S.P.D. 1644, p. 198

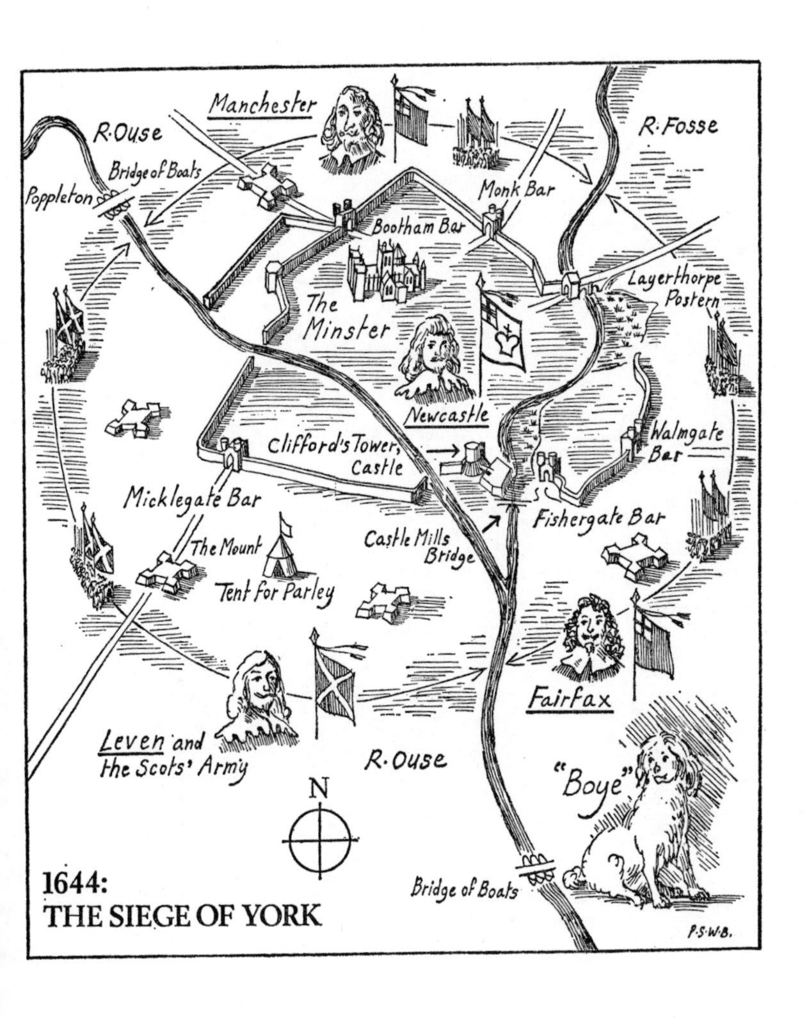

1644:
THE SIEGE OF YORK

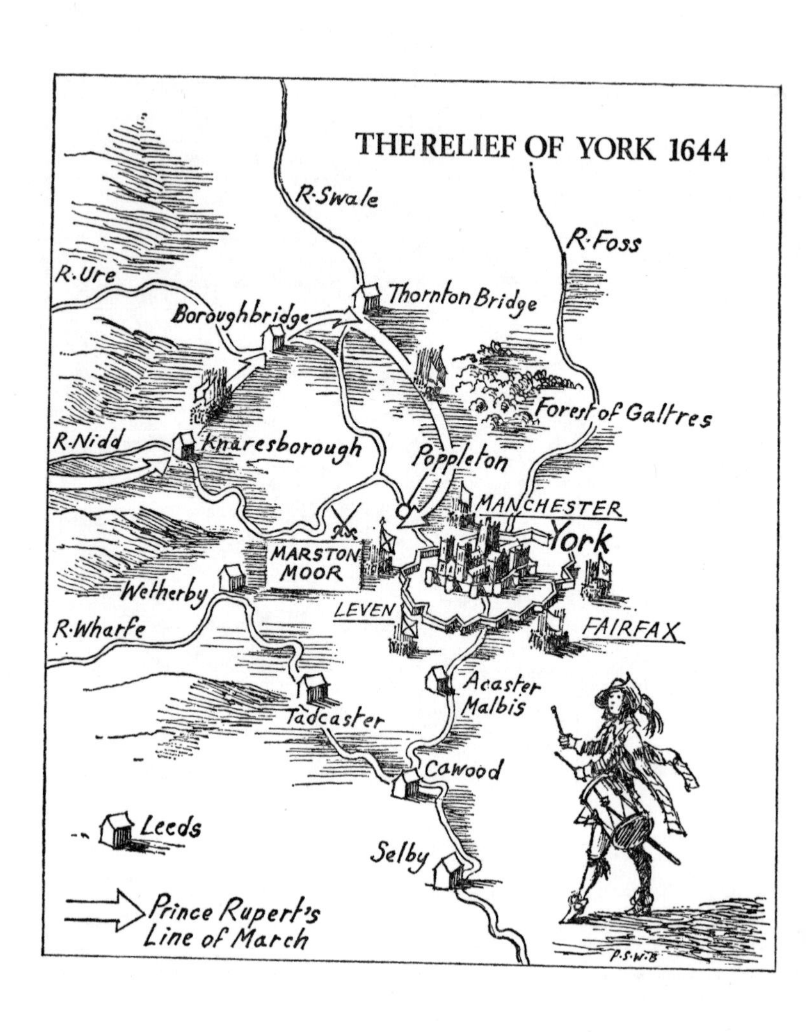
THE RELIEF OF YORK 1644
R·Swale
R·Foss
R·Ure
Thornton Bridge
Boroughbridge
Forest of Galtres
R·Nidd
Knaresborough
Poppleton
MANCHESTER
York
MARSTON MOOR
Wetherby
LEVEN
R·Wharfe
FAIRFAX
Acaster Malbis
Tadcaster
Cawood
Leeds
Selby
Prince Rupert's Line of March
P·S·W·B

York City

Defender:	William Cavendish, Marquis of Newcastle (R)
After Marston Moor:	Sir Thomas Glemham, Governor (R)
Besieger:	Alexander Leslie, Earl of Leven (Scots) Ferdinando, Baron Fairfax (P) (Yorks) Edward Montagu, Earl of Manchester (Eastern Association) (P)
Duration:	21 April–16 July 1643
Outcome:	Surrendered on terms

The ancient town and later city of York was originally established by the Romans as a fortress, garrisoned by the Ninth Legion in AD 71, occupying as a defensive position the spur of land formed by the juncture of the Rivers Ouse and Foss.

The town was sited on the south bank of the Ouse and became sufficiently important to be visited by the Emperors Hadrian, Severus and Constantius. It was occupied by the Danes in AD 876 and by the Normans in 1069. The latter threw up their customary palisaded mound and ditch fortifications over the positions of the, by now, ruined Roman walls.

Two wooden castles were built, one on each side of the Ouse, and between the years 1250 and 1300 a major garrison town had been established, covering a densely populated area of 263 acres. The castle in the east had been rebuilt in stone, it and its bailey being surrounded by a deep and wide moat fed from the Foss. Today's Clifford's Tower is the sole remnant surviving. Its companion in the west has totally disappeared, leaving only the mound known today as the Baile Hill.

The stone walls that still exist, appearing much as they did in the Civil War, are the product of the Middle Ages and are over 3½ miles in circumference. The main roads that entered the city passed through four great gatehouses or bars. Micklegate spanned the road to the south, Bootham that to the north, Monk the Scarborough route and Walmgate that to Hull. Each was provided with a massive tower, great gates, portcullis and barbican. These were supplemented by six small posterns,

North Street, Lendal, Layerthorpe, Fishergate, Castlegate and Skeldergate. To further strengthen the wall, it was pierced at irregular intervals by small towers. For the majority of the circumference the walls were built on the Norman mound and thus were tall and formidable, but from Fishergate Postern to Red Tower they were founded on a pre-Norman mound and were lower. A moat varying in width and depth surrounded the walls and was usually full of water. Rather surprisingly the wall did not exist at all on the east side between Red Tower and Layerthorpe Postern, a distance of about a quarter mile; in its stead was a stretch of low lying ground, flooded since 1068 when the Normans had dammed the River Foss just above the eastern castle to form a formidable obstacle. This area was known as the King's Fishpool.

A few score houses huddled outside the walls round each bar, while on the north-west face, between Bootham Bar and the Ouse was the Abbey of St Mary's, occupying about 10 acres and surrounded by stout walls on three sides. Ridsdale Tate's drawing of York gives an excellent idea of how the city appeared in the fifteenth century.

The Siege

So far we have pictured a formidable, fortified city, but 70 years of peace prior to the Civil War had led to deterioration of the defences, and the citizens had used the moat as an open drain and rubbish tip. Elsewhere it was blocked with weeds and was prone to dry up in hot weather. The keep of the castle (Clifford's Tower) was in a ruinous state, as was the Abbey Church of St Mary's which had suffered at the Dissolution in 1539, though the Abbey's walls still stood.

These disturbing facts were rather tardily realised after the Second Bishop's War with the Scots in 1640 and recommendations were made to put the city in a 'posture of defence'.[1] As the cost was wholly to be borne by the citizens it is hardly surprising that nothing was done. But then as now, when war looms and the public safety is threatened money is speedily made available where there seemed to be none before.[2]

After a five-month stay in York, Charles I came to Nottingham where he raised his standard on 22 August 1642. On 2 September Henry, Earl of Cumberland, was ordered to repair York's defences and put it in a state of war 'and on the next day was ordnance mounted on the Barrs'.[3] With the imminence of danger, 800 townsmen and 800 countrymen were put to work, strengthening the walls and constructing earthworks and ditches within the city, for it was intended to contest the issue street by street if need be. The trained bands were also put on the alert. Anyone desiring to obtain more detailed information may read Drake who states 'the city was everywhere strongly fortified and above twenty cannon great and small planted about it . . .'[4] while Hildyard further enlightens us 'This year [1643] Clifford's being exceedingly ruinous, was re-edified and strengthened with fortifications'.[5]

The climate which made a siege of York inevitable was brought about by the disastrous enterprise embarked upon by Sir John Belasyse, Governor of York, who intercepted despatches from the Fairfaxes which informed him of their plan to unite their forces, which were scattered throughout Yorkshire, and march north to unite with the Scots. Apparently, Belasyse considered this to be a good opportunity to smash the Northern Parliament Army at one blow before they could effect their link-up and he marched out with 3000 of the York garrison, leaving only 1000 behind to defend the city. On 11 April he was defeated at Selby, with the loss of 100 officers and 2000 men, being himself captured.[6]

The news reached the Marquis of Newcastle at Durham on 16 April and, realising the danger that threatened under-garrisoned York, he abandoned Durham and set out on a forced march, hoping to reach the city before his opponents did.

Meanwhile the Fairfaxes had effected a juncture with Leven's Scottish Army at Tadcaster and both armies, totalling about 20000 men, set out for York where they arrived and took up siege positions between 21 and 23 April. 'This year on 23 April, the Scots faced York at a distance, on the west bank of the River Ouse.'[7] That is to say the Scots' line stretched from the Ouse, north-west of the city, until it met the river again south of York near Fulford. Leven's headquarters were at Middlethorpe, most probably at the Manor.

The two Fairfax sectors occupied an area from the east bank of the Ouse at Fulford to about the Red Tower which, as we have seen, was on the edge of the marshy King's Pool. It is considered likely that Lord Fairfax's headquarters were at Heslington Hall.

It seems apparent that the north side of the city was open until the Earl of Manchester arrived with the Army of the Eastern Association five weeks later. 'Thus we were blockt up upon two sides of ye town, and ye rest we had open for about 3 [sic] weeks until such time as my Ld. Manchester came with his Norfolk men',[8] although it seems incredible to suggest that the northern sector was not at least under the surveillance of patrols of horse.

Despite the preparations that had been made to provision the city and to provide fodder for the horse, Newcastle had written to the King for aid on 18 April.[9]

Until the arrival of Manchester during the first week in June the action had been limited to skirmishes – mere trials of strength – on both sides. But when the Eastern Association Army arrived, matters proceeded in earnest. A bridge of boats was constructed north of the city, spanning the Ouse so that the armies could easily contact one another.

Simeon Ashe and William Goade, Chaplains to the Earl of Manchester, could not have conceived the value of the service they were doing future historians by keeping a detailed account of the activities of their masters during the campaign. Their role might be likened to the modern war correspondent, for every few days they sent despatches to London which were speedily printed and sold to the public. They observe (5 June) 'Upon Wednesday most of the Scotts regiments and all the Earle of Manchester's were drawne forth in nearer approaches to the towne . . . whilst the Lord Fairfax with his forces raised a battery within less than musquet shot of the towne upon a hill westward . . .'. The consequence of these moves is shown by Slingsby: '5 pieces of cannon . . . playes continuously into the town, they come nearer to us and takes ye suburbs w(i)t(h)out Waingate [Walmgate] barre and plants 2 pieces in ye street against ye barre'.

Shortly after, Fairfax's men commenced mining under Walmgate Bar from 'a little house on the north of the said gate', but this was discovered in time because a prisoner 'being strictly examined by the Lieutenant Colonel in Cliffords Tower confessed'. Glemham, 'that gallant and vigilant Governor', promptly counter-mined and 'poured water in on them'.[10]

The noose was being drawn ever tighter about the city for on 7 June Baillie comments: 'they within put all the suburbs in a fyre . . . we are now within pistol shot of the walls and are making readie to storm it . . . it cannot be but a bloodie business'.[11] Hildyard says 'Most of the suburbs of the city were burned down except a few houses without Micklegate . . . Moncke Bridge and the Bridge at Lathrop (Layerthorpe] Postern were broken down'.[12]

It must have seemed to Newcastle that his only salvation was the arrival of a relief force, and so to delay the forthcoming attack he procrastinated, offering to parley. Letters passed back and forth between himself and the three Parliament commanders and the time between 8 and 15 June was spent in this way. Realising that Newcastle's sole purpose was to play for time, the preparations for the assault were pressed forward vigorously. It was proposed to explode two mines simultaneously, at Walmgate Bar and St Mary's Tower, and also to attack the city at two other points.

This plan miscarried as the mine at St Mary's was exploded prematurely and Lieutenant General Laurence Crauford's men poured through the breach. Because the attack was unco-ordinated, 300 men were cut off and lost.[13] This sharp lesson seems to have taken the edge off the besiegers' ardour and between 16 June and 1 July the activity was slight, due also to the fact that sickness was rife in the Scots' camp and Fairfax was short of powder, shot, small arms and pay for his men.

Meanwhile, Rupert was advancing to the relief of York. His progress may be judged by the following itinerary:

18 June Lathom House
26 June Skipton
29 June Denton Hall (Sir Thomas Fairfax's residence)
30 June Knaresborough

By a ruse the wily Prince persuaded the numerically superior enemy that his intention was to assault them from the west. This caused them to raise the siege and wait for him, in battle array, concentrated on the villages of Long Marston, Tockwith and Hessay, only to find that he had in fact crossed the Ouse north of the city by the convenient bridge of boats constructed by Manchester. The garrison were not immediately notified of the arrival of Rupert's force; in fact, it would seem that they only found out by accident.

Slingsby tells us that they could not believe that their long-looked-for delivery had happened: 'we were still in some doubt, till we perceiv'd that ye Scots had drawn off their guards, w(h)ich our Centinells gave us notice of'.[14] The Prince sent his chief of cavalry, Lord George Goring, into the city, instructing the Marquis of Newcastle that he intended to bring the enemy to battle the following day (2 July) and ordering him to be ready to march at four o'clock in the morning.

Reluctantly, Newcastle obeyed these orders, but so tardily that he did not arrive on the field until four o'clock in the afternoon, leaving only three regiments to defend York. The description of battles not being within the scope of this book, it is only necessary to comment that Marston Moor was the biggest conflict of the Civil War, not less than 50000 men being involved.[15] Starting in a thunderstorm and ending under a harvest moon, the results were catastrophic for the Royalist cause, for at one stroke they lost not only their Northern Army but the North itself.

All night long the weary refugees came pouring back into York, spreading alarm amidst garrison and townsfolk alike. Rupert rode out next morning 'with the remaining horse and as many footmen as he could force, leaving ye rest in York . . .'.[16] Declaring that he could not bear the laughter of the court, Newcastle, accompanied by 'twenty more of good ranke',[17] abandoned the city, turning over his authority to Sir Thomas Glemham, the Governor. Taking ship at Scarborough, he landed in Hamburg, returning only at the Restoration.

On Thursday 4 July the siege was resumed. New batteries were placed and preparations were made for early storming. By 11 July all was ready for the assault when the garrison asked for a parley. Beyond hope of relief, all that could be hoped for was an honourable surrender.

On Saturday 13 July Sir William Constable and Colonel Lambert were sent by Lord Fairfax into the city to negotiate, after hostages for their safety were given.[18] Spending a whole day in discussion, these officers reported that the garrison requested that commissioners should be appointed 'to treat and conclude upon Articles for the peaceable surrender of the Citie'.

The terms are given in full by Wenham,[19] and it is pleasing to note that the honours of war awarded by one brave adversary to another were granted; the garrison 'shall march out of the Citie on horse back, flying colours, drums beating, Matches lighted at both ends, bullets in their mouths and with all their bag and baggage'.

REFERENCES

1 Rushworth, *Historical Collections*, pp. 1293–4, reporting the recommendations of Lord Herbert

2 *Ibid*

3 Hildyard, *A List or Catalogue of all the Mayors of Yorke . . .*, 1644, in Torre, *The Antiquities of York City* collected from the papers of Christopher Hildyard . . . , 1719, p. 54

4 Drake, *Eboracum: or the History of the Antiquities of the City of York*, 1736, p. 62
5 Hildyard, p. 55
6 *A victorious conquest near Selby in Yorkshire certified by a letter from Lord Fairfax, his quarters . . .*, 1644
7 Hildyard, p. 56
8 *The Diary of Sir Henry Slingsby of Scriven, Bart*, ed. Parsons, 1836, p. 107
9 Warburton, *Memoirs of Prince Rupert and the Cavaliers*, including their private correspondence, 1849, Vol. II, pp. 433–4
10 Hildyard, pp. 58–9
11 *The Letters and Journals of Robert Baillie A.M. Principle of the University of Glasgow 1637–1662* Ed. Laing, 1841, p. 193
12 Hildyard, p. 59
13 Letter from Manchester dated 18 June, 'Leaguer before York' C.S.P.D. 1644, p. 246
14 *Slingsby*, pp. 110–11
15 A full account may be found in Young, *Marston Moor*, 1970
16 *Slingsby*, p. 114
17 *Ibid*
18 *The Kingdomes Weekly Intelligencer*, No. 6
19 Wenham, *The Great and Close Siege of York*, 1970, p. 94

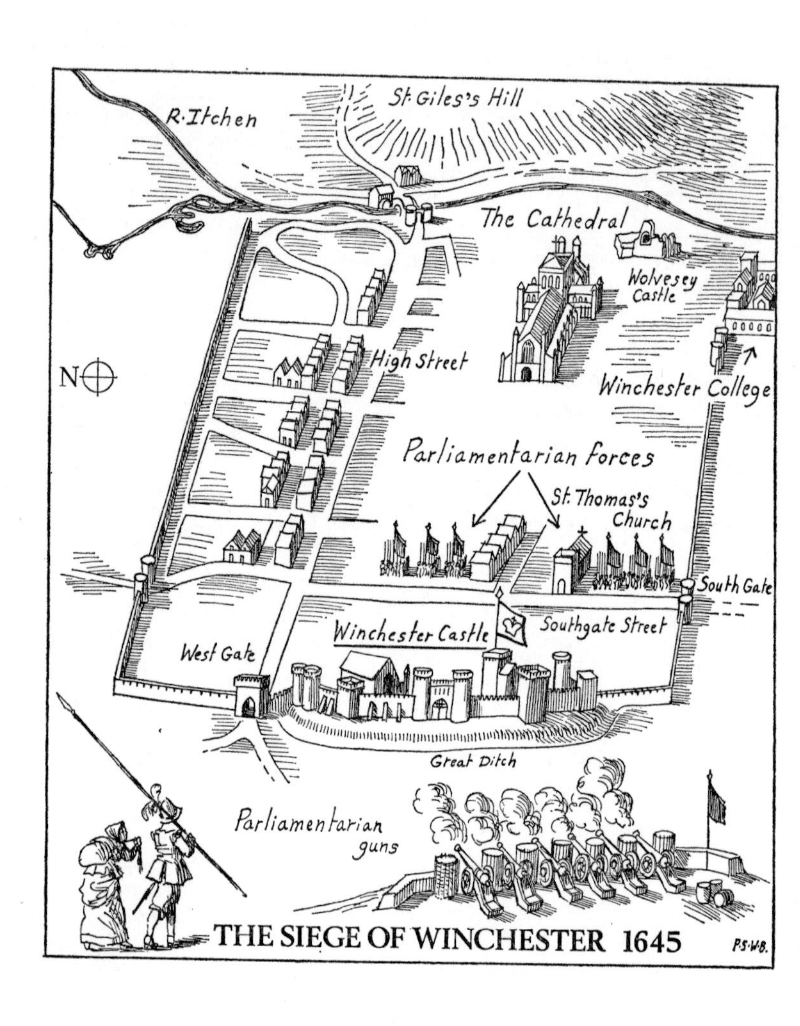

THE SIEGE OF WINCHESTER 1645

Winchester Castle

Defender: Lord Ogle (R)
Besieger: Lieutenant General Oliver Cromwell (P)
Duration: Eight days (28 September–6 October 1645)
Outcome: Surrendered on terms

Winchester ranks as one of the most historical cities in the country. Settled by the Iron Age, it was the chief town of the Belgae whose name was perpetuated by the Romans who called it Venta Belgarum. What defences there were in the native period is not known, but the conquerors surrounded 138 acres with $1\frac{1}{2}$ miles of wall, nine feet wide at the base, built of flint rubble and faced with knapped flints set in a buff-coloured mortar in about AD 200.

The Saxon kings of England, whose capital it was, dwelt in the flat marshy land around the Cathedral but Norman William entrenched himself on the rising ground overlooking the town, no doubt mistrusting the citizens' intentions. His stronghold, large for the time, consisted of two wards backing on to the west front of the town walls.

Little or nothing of his work remains, but the castle retained its importance up to the Civil War, each successive monarch adding to or modifying the fortifications to bring them into line with the latest military innovations of the day. Speed's map of 1606 shows, in a bird's-eye view of the city, that, although joined to the city wall, it was a self-contained unit. Of the two baileys, the inner one was the smaller. At its north-west corner was the mighty keep, a great square tower of flint rubble work, while lesser towers stood at the three other angles. Entrance to the bailey was obtained through a tower in the dividing wall. The outer bailey was protected by three towers. A later engraving,[1] gives a very useful ground level view of the castle, the west or outer walls being furnished with a three-storey gatehouse, its towers being joined by a two-storey chamber, probably containing a portcullis. From the east, viewed from near Saint Thomas' Church inside the town, it has not half the strength, there being no ditch, just a lofty mound, with a long stretch of the wall lacking a defensive tower.

Visible above the walls in both views is the roof of the Great Hall completed by Henry III in 1235, the only considerable part of the castle still in existence. The finest example of a thirteenth-century aisled hall still extant, it has seen much of the pageant of English history. Here Edward held his first court after returning from the Crusades in 1274, and here a number of Plantagenet Parliaments gathered. Here too, Henry V declared war on France, Henry VIII entertained the Emperor Charles V, and his daughter, Mary, held a state reception after her marriage to Philip of Spain.

The Rolls of the twelfth and thirteenth centuries mention other buildings including four chapels, the King's, Queen's, Prince's, Wainscotted, Rosamund's and the Clergy's Chambers and also the chamber where the King (Henry II) was born.

Milner estimates that the castle was about 850 feet in length north to south, while from west to east it was 250 feet in breadth, the great keep being about 100 feet square. The ditch that surrounded it varied in depth but at the keep was supposed to be 100 feet deep. After it was surrendered to Cromwell in 1645 the castle was systematically destroyed, three years being occupied in the task, only the hall being spared.

In the thirteenth century, the Roman town walls being ruinous they were reconstructed largely on the lines of the original. Built of flint and chalk set in a pale mortar, they were said to be seven feet thick and needed repair a century later.[2] Today, little remains of these defences, the greatest stretch being that bounding Wolvesey Castle and two or three minor fragments remaining in private gardens. Of the five gates (depicted on the city's arms), only two remain – the Westgate, a glorious fourteenth-century survival, and the more mundane Kingsgate with a tiny chapel dedicated to St Swithin over it. The destruction here cannot be blamed on Cromwell but rather on eighteenth-century greed and commercial expediency.

The north and south gates were demolished in 1771 by order of the municipal authorities. Because of 'the lowness of the structures of the arches of the said gates whereby a tun of straw and hay cannot be brought in . . . foot passengers have been hindered from passing to and fro . . . by the passage of carriages', so they had to go. Much of the wall was removed by enterprising gentlemen, one of whom, it was mentioned, should 'have liberty to take down as much of the Old City Wall Northward from the Westgate of the City . . . and shall have the materials for his Trouble and Expence'. Not for the first time that history has been laid on the altar of commerce.

The Siege

On 26 September 1645, Lieutenant General Oliver Cromwell was commanded to reduce the garrisons still held for the King in Hampshire. Setting out from Devizes with 2000 horse and three regiments of foot,[3] he arrived at Winchester on 28 September and lost no time in summoning the city, writing to the Mayor, William Longland, in these terms:

> Sir I come not into this city but with a full resolution to save the inhabitants thereof from ruin. I have commanded the soldiers under pain of death that no wrong be done which I shall strictly observe; only I expect you to give me entrance unto the city; without necessitating me to force my way; which if I do then it will not be in my power to save you or it. I expect your answer in half an hour and rest
>
> Your servant
>
> Winton September 28 1645 Oliver Cromwell
>
> 5 oc. at night.

The reply that the Mayor returned was conciliatory but procrastinating,[4] stating that it was not in his power to yield up the city because the Royalist commander, Lord Ogle, was Governor but that he would try to persuade Ogle to surrender castle and city. Next day Cromwell, not to be denied, entered the city.[5] Having notice that Dr Curle, Bishop of Winchester, was in residence, he offered him a safe conduct in deference to his office, but Curle, seemingly suspicious of his intentions, refused and took refuge in the castle. A further summons to Ogle to surrender the stronghold being refused, work started on preparations for a siege.[6] Some of the guns being out of action, it was Friday 3 October before the batteries were ready to fire and, having fired one round, a third summons to surrender was sent in, and again refused.

The castle was surrounded by the Parliament forces. One party covered the east front from an open space inside the walls, while another was in the city to the north. The guns had not battered at the walls long when Ogle had a change of heart, and he was in the act of negotiating with the Roundheads when he again changed his mind and broke off the transactions. All the next day the Parliament guns roared unceasingly, one after another, as quickly as they could charge and discharge.[7] In one single day 200 shots were fired at the castle walls.[8] They 'threw in grenadoes which did very much execution, one of them broke into the Great Hall and killed three men'. A breach wide enough for 30 men to march abreast through was made near 'a Black

Tower', which Cromwell thought stormable. When the evening fell, Ogle apparently realised that continued resistance would only see the castle beaten to pieces round his ears, and achieve nothing, so he wrote this letter to Cromwell:

Sir, I have received formerly a letter from you wherein you desire, to avoid the effusion of Christian blood, to which you received my answer that I was as willing as yourself. But having no reply to advance your desires I have thought fit to desire a treaty whereby we might pitch up some means both for the affecting of that and the preservation of this place, and that I might receive your letter with all convenience I desire that neither officer nor soldier of your party may come off their guards and I shall take like course with mine.

Ogle,

Winton Castle at 8 at night October 5 1645

Cromwell thereupon sent in Colonel Hammond and Major Harrison to draw up articles of surrender which, after a discussion lasting most of the night, were agreed. Hugh Peters, Cromwell's Chaplain, when he inspected the castle after the Royalists had marched out, found 'the Castle was manned by 700 men . . . the chief men I saw there were Viscount Ogle, Sir John Pawlet [Paulet] an old soldier, Sir William Courtny, and Colonel Bennet, also Dr Curle and his chaplain in their long cassocks'.[9] He enumerates the spoil '4 great pieces of ordnance, 3 lesser pieces, 17 barrels of powder, 2000 lbs, weight of musket bullets, 800 weight of match, 700 muskets, 200 pikes, halberds and other weapons'. After cataloguing a vast store of food sufficient to feed an army, he finishes off with '142 hogsheads of strong beer, 70 dozen candles with divers pictures and Popish crucifixes'. If it might appear that Ogle was somewhat faint-hearted to render up a stronghold which was so well provided, and with so little resistance, it might also seem that Cromwell was fortunate, which fact he was aware of for he wrote 'His [God's] goodness in this is much to be acknowledged for the Castle was well manned . . . the works were exceeding good and strong. It is likely that it would have cost much blood to have taken by storm'.[10]

REFERENCES

1 See Milner, *History of Winchester*, Vol. 2, where it appears as a footnote to the engraving of the King's House, designed by Wren but never completed

2 Cunliffe, *The Winchester City Wall*, City of Winchester Museums and Library Committee, p. 69
3 *Perfect Passages*, 1 October 1645
4 For the full text see Bailey, *Transcripts from the Municipal Archives*, 1856, p. 148
5 *Exact Journal*, 1 October 1645
6 Cromwell's report to Fairfax, 1645
7 *Ibid*
8 Hugh Peter's Report to House of Commons, 1645
9 *Ibid*
10 Cromwell's report

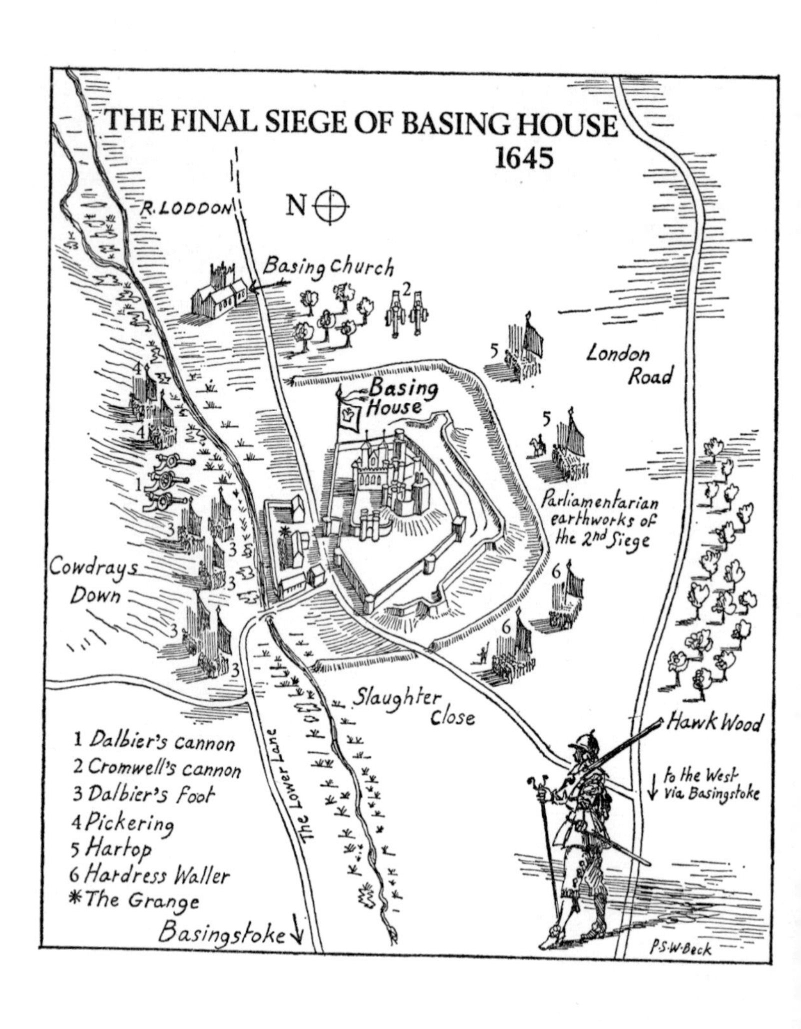
THE FINAL SIEGE OF BASING HOUSE
1645
R. LODDON
N
Basing Church
Basing House
London Road
Parliamentarian earthworks of the 2nd Siege
Cowdrays Down
Slaughter Close
The Lower Lane
Hawk Wood
to the West via Basingstoke
1 Dalbier's cannon
2 Cromwell's cannon
3 Dalbier's Foot
4 Pickering
5 Hartop
6 Hardress Waller
* The Grange
Basingstoke
P.S.W. Beck

Basing House (Aimez Loyaute)

Defender: John Paulet, Marquis of Winchester (R)
Besiegers: Colonel Richard Norton (P)
(Raid) 31 July 1643
(1) Sir William Waller (P), 7 November 1643
(2) Colonel Richard Norton, 11 July 1644
(3) Colonel John Dalbier (P), 20 August 1645
(4) Lieutenant General Oliver Cromwell (P), 8 October 1645
Duration: (1) Nine days
(2) 25 weeks
(3/4) Seven weeks and three days
Outcome: (1) Abandoned siege
(2) Relieved by Colonel Henry Gage (R)
(3/4) House stormed and burnt 4 October 1645

Basing House in 1643 was as massive a place as any in the kingdom, covering 14½ acres, second only in size to the great castle at Windsor. Its owner, John Paulet, 5th Marquis of Winchester, was reputed to be one of the richest landowners in the country.

Basing owed its transformation from unremarkable country manor to palace fortress to Sir William Paulet who became successively Lord St John of Basing and 1st Marquis of Winchester. He possessed the enviable and somewhat unusual ability to tread the tightrope of power and favour throughout the reigns of four Tudor sovereigns and not only kept his head but accumulated vast wealth and influence.

Under King Henry VIII, Paulet was Comptroller and Treasurer of the Household, an appointment he also held under King Edward VI and Queen Elizabeth I. When he inherited Basing it was a miscellany of buildings dating from Norman times onward, enclosed in an earthwork ring, said to be of Iron Age origin but most certainly heightened and strengthened by the Norman Adam de Porte, who fought at Hastings. It was he who created the palisaded bailey, still to be seen today in its later form. Over the years 1530–70 Paulet caused the earthwork to be lined with brick within and without.

All the buildings were to be modified in the latest style and the entrance to the earthwork blocked by a mighty four-storeyed brick gatehouse with towers. Even today, after the devastation of fire and demolition, one can discern the handsome Tudor brick superimposed on the Norman stonework.

Hardly was this work completed than this tireless builder erected, alongside this 'Old House', (or castle as it was sometimes called) a giant five-storey 380-roomed 'New House', part palace, part fortress.

From the three engravings still intact, of which the best is by Wenceslaus Hollar (1607–77) who served in the garrison during the siege, it is shown to have had a great tower in the north-east corner with projecting turrets and another in the south-west corner. Both houses were surrounded by a deep dry moat and were enclosed at a distance by a common defensive wall nine feet thick, brick faced with a rammed earthen core. This was almost a mile in circumference. At intervals there were brick towers, one of them a dovecote housing 500 birds. Of these defences only the north face remains in a sufficient state of preservation to give an impression of the original appearance of the whole.

The north front was partially covered by a large farmhouse known as the Grange. Enclosing this with its huge barn and out-buildings was a high buttressed wall, several bricks thick, by no means as sturdy as the main walls, but capable of being defended. While the present farmhouse which stands on the site is not contemporary with the siege, the great barn is, and by way of credentials, still bears the marks of the struggle all along its huge loophooled length. In addition, the whole north front had natural defences as the Marquis's siege diary shows. 'The Grange is severed [from the House] by a wall and a common road again divided from Cowdrays Down by meades, rivulets and a river [the Loddon] running from Basingstoke a mile distant.'[1] Marshes filled the valley here, the 'lower road' from the village to the town must have been mirey in the extreme.

A Roundhead soldier's opinion of the house was later expressed thus: 'The place is very strongly fortified. The walls are made thick and strong to bear out cannon bullets and the house built upright so that no man can command the roof. The windows are guarded by the outer walls . . . the house is as large and spacious as the Tower of London and strongly walled about . . . besides they have great stores of both ammunition and victual to serve for a long time and in the wall divers pieces of ordnance about the House'.[2]

The Sieges

The Marquis's diary suggests that he was much inclined to neutrality in the struggle between King and Parliament, but by the very nature of his position and rank he had eventually to choose one or the other.

Irritated by a number of minor attacks, perhaps by the citizens of Basingstoke, who were of Parliamentary sympathies, he petitioned the King in July 1643 to garrison the house. Hardly had he done so than an attack was mounted by Colonel Richard Norton who lived at Alresford. Knowing the Marquis's wealth and appreciating the strategic value of the house, commanding the great road from London to the west, he brought up a troop of horse (St Barbe's) and one of dragoons (Cole's) expecting an easy prey.

Unfortunately for him, his arrival coincided with that of the troops sent from Oxford to do garrison duty, under Lieutenant Colonel Robert Peake, whose service at the house was to earn him a knighthood, seconded by several troops of horse under Colonel Sir Henry Bard, who with little effort sent the Roundheads pell-mell back to Farnham Castle

For a time all was quiet and the garrison made the most of it by reinforcing the weak south and west faces of the stronghold with earthworks.[3] In the first place the defences were just a great bank, four or five feet high but later in the war bastions were added at the corners.

The first of the three major attacks was mounted by Sir William Waller on 6 November 1643. With the addition of three regiments of the London trained bands which rendezvoused with him at Farnham, his force consisted of 16 troops of horse, five companies of dragoons, 36 companies of foot and a train of artillery.[4] The garrison at this time numbered about 400.

Waller sited his guns on Cowdray's Down, the rising ground to the north of the house. He then summoned the Marquis to surrender and, being firmly but courteously denied, opened fire at daybreak on 7 November. He followed up his bombardment with a general assault on the north front stretching from the Grange to the church. The attack on the former was led by Captain Clinson, 'a man of great courage and resolution', who carried his objective with very little loss, whence 'having steady aim at the holes and sighting from easy places, they much annoyed the garrison'.

The difficulties encountered further to the left of the line were mainly due to the fact that the garrison had put to the torch all the cottages that might have given cover to the attackers, one of whom wrote, 'Our Army had no shelter not so much as a hovel . . . yet this did nothing to discourage their resolution.'[5] However, *Mercurius Aulicus* reports that 'they took shelter in the ruins that remained from which they poured a well sustained fire of musketry, all the while the guns battered away at the Castle and New House'.

But about 3 p.m. the wind rose bringing a rainstorm in its wake dampening both the men's powder and their ardour, which 'made the army sound a retreat, which to give them content, Sir William Waller retreated about half a mile to refresh them'.[6] They retired to the cold comfort of their billets in the fields which as Lieutenant Elias Archer noted 'our lodging and our service did not agree, the one being so hot, the other so cold'. After waiting in vain for the weather to abate, Waller withdrew his sodden army to shelter at Basingstoke and the surrounding villages.

Not until 12 November did Waller return to the attack. After a two-hour bombardment at about 2 p.m., the Parliament armies stormed from all sides, giving in the words of Archer 'a hot and desperate charge'.

The main attacks went in from the north and the north-east and it was here that the heavy concentration of foot were deployed with the New House as their objective. A news-sheet commented: 'they hazarded themselves on the very muzzles of the enemy's muskets'.[7] Inside the fortress everyone took part in the desperate defence, even the Marchioness and her ladies standing on the walls of the outhouses showering down bricks, tiles and stones. The attack by 500 Roundheads across the open space of the park was pressed with much less vigour. Apparently the Westminster Auxiliaries[8] found, as have others after them, that there is a great difference between the parade ground and active service. When the cannon opened up on them with case shot, it struck such terror into these untried soldiers that nothing could persuade them to advance further. The attack was maintained until dark, when they withdrew to their cheerless quarters in the fields.

On the 13th the rain turned to sleet and snow and the Parliament Army once again withdrew to dry themselves out. On 14 November, there was a general alarm that Lord Hopton with upwards of 5000 men was advancing on Basing from Andover, and when his advanced picquets made contact with the Royalist scouts, Waller withdrew his troops to Farnham, 'Having bruised and dishonoured his army' as the siege diary puts it.

It was not until 11 July 1644 that the house was again beleaguered, this time by Colonel Richard Norton whose early attempt had been so providently thwarted. Knowing of Waller's inability to take the place by storm, he decided to starve the garrison out and encircled the site with breastworks and batteries. His force was formidable, consisting of five Surrey companies under Sir Richard Onslow, Colonel Herbert Morley with six companies from Sussex, two companies of Colonel Jones's Greencoats from the garrison of Farnham Castle, and his own force: a regiment of foot and one of horse to which were later added three more troops of horse, in all about 200 men.

Morley's pikemen and musketeers blanketed the southern approaches, Onslow's, on the right of Morley's, covered the lower lane and the area in between while guards of horse completed the circle by continually patrolling in between. The result of this blockade soon made itself felt: flour became short, there being no mill to grind corn,[9] and presently even corn itself became scarce. Salt and other necessities were exhausted. This grim and constant squeeze by Norton was more to be feared than all Waller's cannon.

But the besiegers did not rely only upon famine. It was reported that 'two mortar pieces were sent to Basing this day, and divers grenadoes which we hope will provide good instruments for the gaining of Basing House, for we are certified that the besiegers have entrenched themselves firmly'.[10]

Heavy artillery had been brought up and sited. As time wore on the breastworks crept little by little towards the walls of Basing House and the siege diary states they were 'within half a musket shot'. Some time about 28 July the mortars arrived and opened fire with 36-pound stone shot into the stronghold. Sallies were made out of the house on a limited, though successful, basis, despite the fact that the garrison now consisted of only 250 men. The Marquis wrote, 'Our necessities grow fast on us, now drinking water and for some weeks making our bread with pease and oats, our stock of wheat being spent'. But still he ignored surrender demands, with the house being pounded to pieces round his ears by the constant bombardment, until in the early part of September he acknowledged the seriousness of his position by sending a desperate message to the Royalist capital at Oxford, stating that he could hold out only for another 10 days, 'then must I submit to the worst conditions the rebels are like to grant my person and religion'.

The Oxford garrison was fully committed but Colonel Henry Gage raised a volunteer force. This consisted of Colonel Hawkins' regiment (the garrison of Greenland House which had recently yielded), 100 recruits, Sir William Campion's horse loaned from Boarstall, and in addition 'the Lords mounted their servants upon their own horses'. In one of the most gallant exploits of the war, Gage led them through 40 miles of enemy-held territory.

Wearing the orange sash of the Parliament to avoid detection he left Oxford on the night of 9 September 1644 and, impressed by the urgency of the situation, 'he marched forward with as much speed as the foot soldiers could manage until he came by bye lanes to the village of Aldermaston'.

Here the true colours of the force was shown, for an advance party, coming upon a Roundhead patrol, momentarily forgot they were masquerading as Parliamentary soldiers and engaged them, killing one and capturing another six. What Gage said to the impetuous officer in charge may only be guessed at, but recriminations were useless, for in the time it took a horse to gallop to Basing, Colonel Norton knew of the approach of the relief force.

In the early morning of 11 September Gage and his tired men arrived in the vicinity of the House and after a desperate struggle cut their way through the besiegers to deliver their precious load of gunpowder and match. The garrison, thus reinforced, opened a way through to Basingstoke and kept it open while Gage entered the town. It was market day and despite the black scowls of the townsfolk he commandeered '100 cattle whereof divers were excellent fat oxen, as many more sheep and forty and odd hogs'. All day long according to his report he 'continued to send as much wheat, malt, salt, oats, bacon, cheese as I could get carts to transport'.

Returning to Oxford presented even greater danger than the outward journey, and might have seemed an impossibility to a lesser man. But Gage's ingenuity was equal to the task and he slipped out of Basing 'without sound of drum or trumpet' under cover of darkness and fog. The enemy were gathered along his line of retreat in strength, but amazingly he avoided them, swimming his horses across the Kennet at Burghfield and the Thames at Pangbourne, and arriving at Wallingford on 13 September and Oxford on the following day. For this exploit Gage gained a well-deserved knighthood.

But Norton was not long to be held at bay. By 23 September he had recaptured the church and closed the circle once again.[11] Then, on 22 October, the watchers in Basing's lofty towers saw an unforgettable sight when three Parliament armies passed by, marching towards

Newbury where they hoped to crush the King's outnumbered army once and for all.

In the second battle of Newbury, the Roundhead pincer attacks were ill-co-ordinated, and the result was inconclusive. Leaving his artillery and valuables in Donnington Castle, Charles fell back on Oxford during the night, returning on 9 November with all due ceremony 'beating drums, colours flying and trumpets prattling', reinforced by Rupert, to recover his goods from the castle.

Clarendon tells that 'his [the King's] heart was set upon the relief of Basing, which was again distressed', and after deliberation it was decided that a thousand horse under Colonel Sir Henry Gage should be detached from the Royalist Army and that each trooper should take 'each a bag of corn or other provision and march so as to be at Basing House the next morning'. But there proved to be no need to cut their way through as anticipated, for on the day before Gage arrived, that is on 19 November, Norton, whose 2000 men had been reduced during the siege by desertion, disease and casualties to 700, raised the siege, firing the hutted encampment before retreating once again to Farnham.

When, for the third and final time the house was besieged, the King's fortunes were at a low ebb. Naseby had been fought and lost on 14 June 1645,[12] Charles losing his infantry, guns and most of his baggage. With the defeat of the Royalist Western Army at Langport (10 July) the collapse of the King's cause was imminent. Now all that remained for Parliament to do was to reduce the fortified towns, manor houses and other strongholds that still held out. It might be thought that the Marquis, knowing that there was no hope of relief, would now surrender on the best terms he could get, particularly as a quarrel over religion had resulted in the Protestant Sir Marmaduke Rawdon withdrawing his regiment from the garrison.

The Roundhead 'gentlemen of Hants and Sussex',[13] having examined the tactics and lessons of the two previous sieges, decided it would be as well to use a skilled engineer who would apply a scientific approach to the problem of dealing with the stubborn garrison. Employing a 'cunning engineer', Colonel John Dalbier, a Dutchman with a fine record of service to the Parliamentarian cause, they provided him with 800 horses and foot. On 20 August this force appeared before Basing whose garrison, it may be assumed, were amazed that they committed no hostile act. On 23 August Captain Blagraves' company from Reading joined Dalbier, and later a further 100 musketeers from Southwark arrived.

Still no signs of activity were shown by Dalbier, at which the Royalist news-sheet *Mercurius Aulicus* of 20 August[14] made great sport: 'the engineer fell to his pretence – the work itself is money' it gibed. It seems that Dalbier was making his plans methodically, looking at the structures before him with an engineer's eye, considering how much leverage would need to be applied, and where, to bring about the collapse of the whole fabric.

A month later he had sited his guns and opened fire. The effect of his purposeful cannonade, compared with the random fire of Norton, soon became apparent. Applied to the New House, bricks were first loosened in the main wall, then a long sinuous crack appeared; when the guns were then turned against the huge corner tower it crashed to the ground and 'our men saw beds and bedding and other goods fall into the court'.[15] About this time, too, we hear of the first use of a kind of poison gas. Wet straw impregnated with brimstone and arsenic was set alight, the wind carrying the fumes over the House, though without any known effect!

Lieutenant General Oliver Cromwell, fresh from the intaking of Winchester Castle, arrived at Basing on 8 October 1645.[16] In his train came some of the heaviest siege guns then known, one at least being a Cannon Royal which fired a shot weighing 63 pounds, while two others were demi-cannon which threw a 27-pound shot.

Dalbier's batteries were said to be 'on the other side where he had placed them close to Basing town',[17] that is presumably on Cowdray's Down, while Cromwell's 'great guns . . . were drawn up on the South east of the House',[18] probably in the little wood, the remnants of which still remain at the juncture of the modern Crown Lane and Milking Pen Lane. Cromwell had little time to waste on this small garrison and was impatient to conclude the business. A final crisp demand for surrender being refused, he sited his guns and opened fire on 12 October.

By nightfall, the heavy missiles had breached the walls in at least two places: wide enough to 'let a regiment pass'.[19] At 6 a.m. Tuesday 14 October 1645, the massive strength of the Roundhead Army was thrown against the breaches. Dalbier attacked by the Grange; on his left was Colonel John Pickering, next Hartop's regiment, then Sir Hardress Waller (cousin to Sir William) and on the extreme right Colonel Montague's regiment.

The garrison were too scanty to withstand the weight of the assault and retreated into the two houses. The New House was soon taken, the attackers sliding in through the windows, then through its gateway and thence into Adam de Portes' bailey.

At the gatehouse of the Old House, the garrison still resisted hopelessly but fiercely. Pickering, at the head of his storming party, shouting 'Fall on, fall on, all is ours!',[20] took the gateway and when a wave of Waller's and Montague's men came over the wall, all resistance was at an end.

The plunder of the house amounted to £200,000, a great sum, but still the legend persists of a golden hoard buried in the grounds.[21] Well might Cromwell write to Parliament next day with typical English understatement, calling it 'a good encouragement'. Some time during that day the house caught fire and burned for 20 hours after which time 'nothing was left but bare walls and chimneys'.[22] Even these no longer remain today, for the villagers were encouraged to take away the building materials to rebuild their houses burned in the siege, and many of the old cottages in existence today can be proved to be so built.

REFERENCES

1 *Marquis of Winchester's Siege Diary*, 1644, p. 1
2 *The Soldiers Report Concerning Sir William Waller's fight against Basing House*, [Anon], 1643
3 Suggested by O'Neil in *Castles and Cannon*, 1960, and borne out largely by aerial photographs
4 Archer, *A true relation of the marching of the Red Trained Bands of Westminster, The Green Auxiliaries of London and the Yellow Auxiliaries of the Tower Hamlets*, 1643
5 *The Soldiers Report*
6 *Ibid*
7 *True Informer*, 23 November
8 *Parliament Scout*, 23 November
9 *Siege Diary*
10 *Weekly Account*, 20 July 1644
11 *Siege Diary*
12 Young and Adair, *Hastings to Culloden*, 1964
13 *Mercurius Rusticus*, 14 June 1645
14 *Mercurius Aulicus*, 20 August
15 *Weekly Account*, 1 October
16 *Moderate Intelligencer*, 11 October
17 *Scottish Dove*, No. 104

[18] *Mercurius Verdicus*, 11 October
[19] *Scottish Dove*, No. 104
[20] *Mercurius Civicus*, 22 October
[21] Emberton, *Love Loyalty – the Close and Perilous Siege of Basing House 1643–45*, 1972
[22] *The full and last relation of all things concerning Basing House*, Hugh Peters Report to House of Commons, 1645

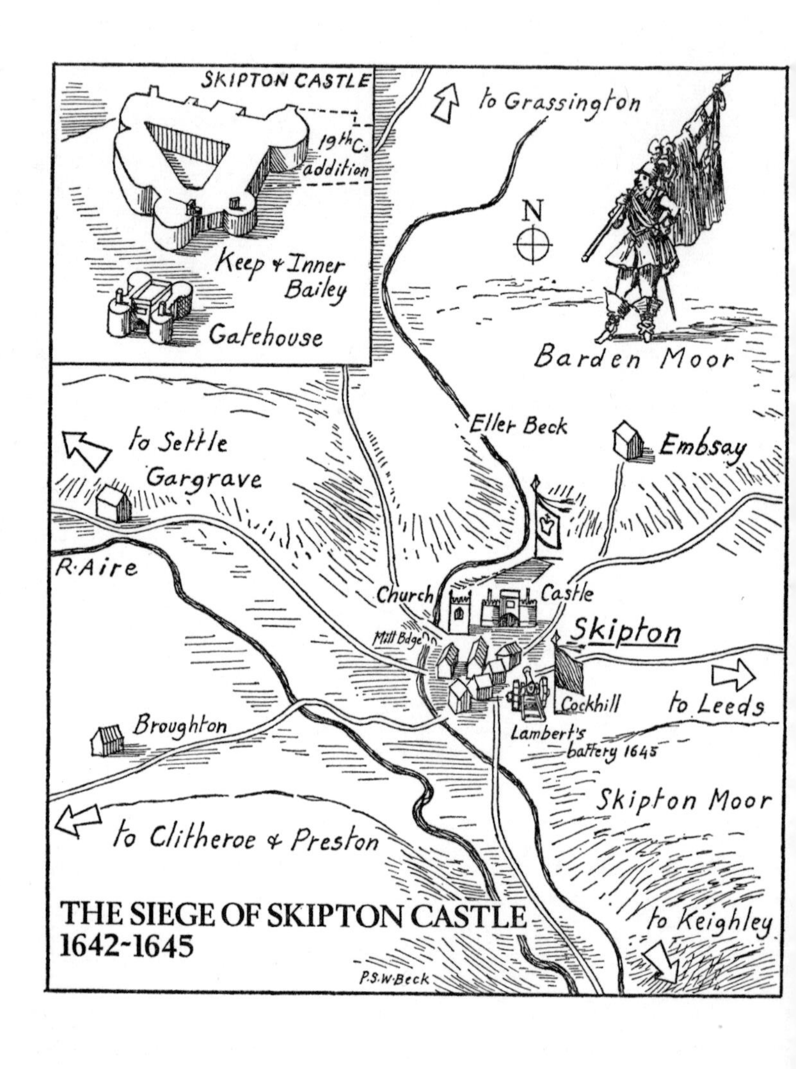

THE SIEGE OF SKIPTON CASTLE
1642-1645

Skipton Castle ('Desormais')

Defender:	Colonel Sir John Mallory (R)
Besieger:	Colonel John Lambert (P) chiefly, although other officers commanded at various times.
Duration:	*c.* 23 December 1642 to 21 December 1645
Outcome:	Surrendered on honourable terms

The history of the town of Skipton (Anglo-Saxon Sceptone, Sheep-town) is very largely the history of the Clifford family who were granted the demesne in 1310 and held it until 1675. The first castle was built by Robert de Romille in the eleventh century. The site was well chosen, being on a rock (which precluded mining), with a steep drop to the moat 120 feet below on the northern aspect, but with a moderate southern declivity. All that remains of his stronghold[1] is a gateway, a vaulted passage and a flanking tower, the remainder dating from the fourteenth to the seventeenth centuries. Other notable features are the great gateway with squat round towers equipped with double gates, the great banqueting hall 50 feet long, a dungeon, and an immense kitchen complete with baking and roasting hearths, the latter being of a size to take a whole ox on the spit. The defensive walls are of such a massive thickness that they contain spiral staircases within them.

The Tudor portion of the castle including a magnificent long gallery and octagonal tower was built by the first Clifford Earl of Cumberland, to celebrate the union of his son with the Lady Eleanore Brandon, a niece of Henry VIII. Skipton was one of the castles in which the unfortunate Mary Queen of Scots was incarcerated, and George, the third Earl was one of the peers who tried her in 1586.

During the Civil War the castle was held for the King, eventually surrendering after a long and honourable resistance. In 1648, Parliament ordered it to be slighted and it was made untenable. Anne, the fourteenth and last Clifford, commenced the work of restoration nine years later. Her work can be seen everywhere, the decorated rainwater heads and other places bearing the initials AP (she was Countess of Pembroke) and family crests. A tablet over the entrance, after naming her style and titles, goes on to state 'this Skipton Castle was repayred . . . in the years 1657 and 1658, after this maine part of itt had laine ruinous ever since

December 1648 . . . Isaiah, Chap. 58 Ver. 12', which verse reads: 'and they that shall be of thee shall build the old waste places, thou shalt raise up the foundations of many generations and thou shalt be called the repairer of the breach . . .'

The Siege

In the autumn of 1642 the King issued his commissions of array, which were useful as a gauge of Loyalty if nothing else. It fell to Henry Clifford, Earl of Cumberland and Lord of the Castle and honour of Skipton, in the capacity of Lord Lieutenant of the County of York to implement the commission and an account of the vigour with which he implemented this task still exists, with a statement of the money[2] raised for the war chest at that time.

Shortly afterwards he was appointed commander of the Yorkshire forces and published a rallying call in the form of a declaration in which the following stirring lines occur: 'though we perish in this worke we shall rest satisfied that we have preserved our Faith and honour untainted, and if all others desert us in this resolution we will not faile ourselves nor our duty to our King and Country . . .'

But it was not to be for 'although [he] was of entire affection to the King [he was] much decayed in the vigour of his body and mind and unfit for the activity of the season',[13] and the command passed to the active Earl of Newcastle.

About the time that the forces of Lord Fairfax, Parliament's commander in the North, clashed with the Royalists at Tadcaster (6 December 1642) it would appear that Skipton Castle was garrisoned for the first time with a force of 300 men under Sir John Mallory, 'a most valiant soldier'.[4] Just as no fixed date can be ascribed to the creation of the garrison, so no exact date can be set to the first skirmish involving it, but it would seem to be in the last week of December, for on 23 December there occurs in the parish register the entry 'Souldier Slayne'.

It was to be the first of many, for although the siege might seem to have been more of a containing operation for the first two years, sallies were frequent and bloody, a notable example being the attack on the Manor House of Thornton in July 1643 by a force under Mallory's deputy, Major John Hughes, in which they captured the house, retaining possession of it for only a short time before it was re-taken and later burned. The parish registers of Thornton record, shortly, 'thirteen soldiers buried 26 July' while those of Skipton of the same date read 'William Gill, a soldier slaine at Thornton'.

Towards the end of 1643 occurred the death of Henry Clifford from an attack of fever.

From the registers it would appear that the interminable skirmishing continued in the early part of 1644, the entries speaking for themselves.

Jan. 19 – a souldier that dyed at Francis Twisletonn's, in Skipton.
Feb. 9 – John Hargraves, a souldier, slaine on top of Rumley's more.
Feb. 12 – Tho. Hall, a trooper, unfortunately slayne by a pistol.
May 17 – Henry Briggs, a souldier.
May 18 – Henry Ashworth, a rebell.
May 22 – Robert Austen, a rebell.
May 24 – Steven Maudsley, a souldier, unfortunately slayne.
May 31 – Tho. Whittecar, a souldier.
June 21 – Edward Walltonn, a souldier, barborusly slayne by the rebells.

The castle's first real appearance in a martial sense on the national scene was on the eve of Marston Moor, when the relieving army of Prince Rupert, arriving on 26 June, stayed at Skipton for three days to give his men 'time to fix their arms' and send messengers into York. Presumably the besiegers, who were by all accounts in no great strength, melted away before the advance of the Royalist Army which consisted of some 14000 men, or perhaps Lambert had already withdrawn them, to strengthen Fairfax's forces when he had received intelligence of Rupert's approach.

The countryside surrounding Skipton is said to have been laid waste by so large an army passing through it, and the Cliffords must have conceived that they had a moral responsibility for some of the damage caused, for in their accounts appears the entry 'Bolton 12 July 1644 – Agreed with Rich. Barnvis for all that piece of ground at Bolton called Hambilton as it now putteth out to be eaten and soiled by the princes horse as they passed thro' this county &c. £20'.

As has been related in a previous chapter, York was relieved on 1 July. The following day Rupert committed his entire strength and that of the garrison in an ill-advised effort to destroy the Allied Armies, culminating in the largest battle ever fought on English soil (except possibly for Towton).

The North was irretrievably lost for the King, and York was doomed at a blow when the Royalist Army was shattered by the disciplined might of Cromwell's Ironsides, admirably supported by the lighter Scots cavalry of David Leslie.

Having commanded the second line of the right wing at Marston Moor, Lambert returned once more to Skipton. It might have been thought that with all hope of relief gone, Fairfax might have given reinforcement to Lambert to bring the siege to a speedy conclusion, but apparently he did not feel that the matter was of sufficient consequence, and so it dragged on.

Towards the end of 1644, the garrison were constantly sending out raiders, 'scarcely a day passed but information was received of irreparable depredations and the most wanton barbarities committed by these parties', in which they were joined by the Royalists of Knaresborough Castle. One of these raids resulted in the death of the deputy governor of the garrison, who led the expedition.

The time when these sallies could be lightheartedly carried out was drawing to a close. One by one the Royalist strongpoints in the North were being compelled to surrender. On 21 July it was Pontefract Castle, on 25 July it was Scarborough, Tickhill the next day, Sandal 2 October, and so the dreary catalogue went on. Small wonder, if hearing this endless tale of disasters, the garrison and its commander became dispirited. Stores and ammunition were becoming depleted and there was no chance of replenishing them. It must have become more and more apparent that further resistance could serve no useful purpose, and so Mallory asked for a parley, and, honourable terms being agreed, the garrison marched out on 21 December 1645.

It is recorded that on 26 December 'this House [Parliament] officially received letters from the North bringing an account of the rendition of the strong garrison of Skipton Castle in Craven which had long been besieged by our forces . . . [this surrender] is one of the greatest importance, for by this means not only all of Yorkshire is cleared and happily reduced to the obedience of Parliament but also all Northumberland, Cumberland, Westmorland and Lancashire'.

REFERENCES

1 Renn, *Norman Castles*, p. 312

[2] See *An abstract of the gentry of Yorkshire who attended King Charles the First att Yorke 1642 with the Summes of Money subscribed from his Service*

[3] See Harbutt-Dawson, *The History of Skipton*, 1882

[4] Young, *Marston Moor*, 1970, p. 56

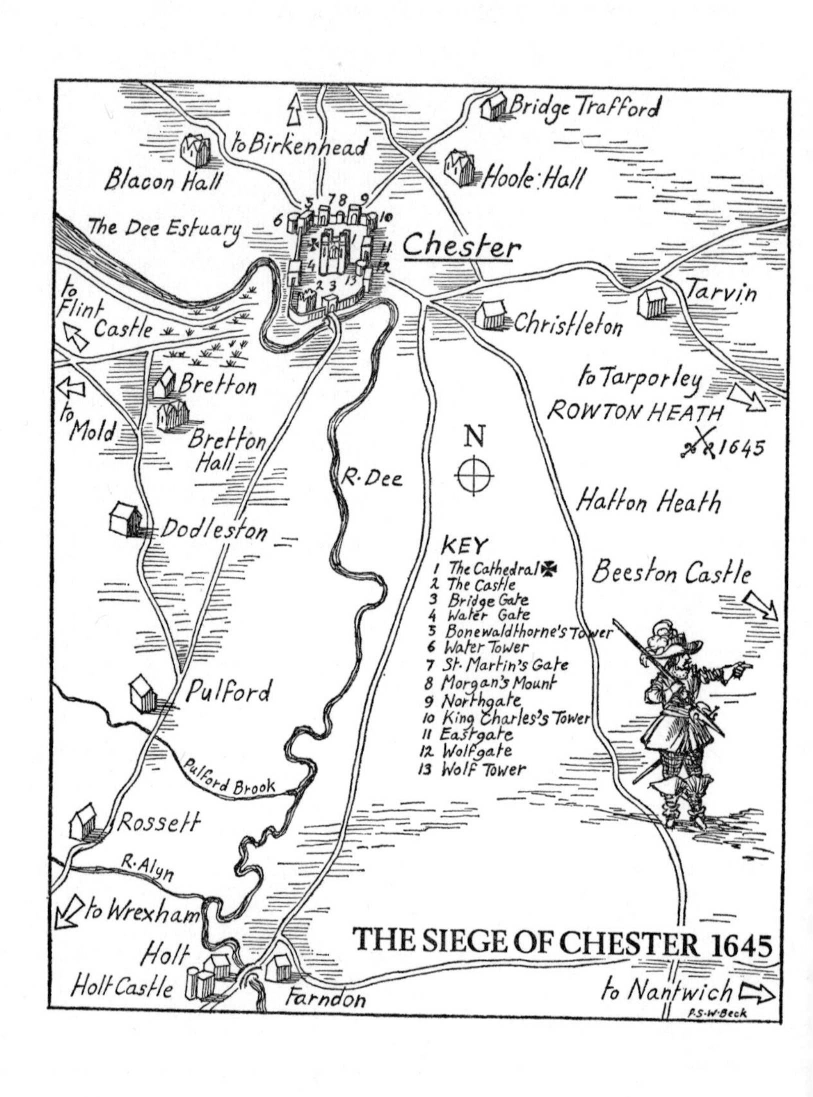
to Birkenhead
Bridge Trafford
Blacon Hall
Hoole Hall
The Dee Estuary
Chester
Tarvin
to Flint Castle
Christleton
Bretton
to Mold
Bretton Hall
to Tarporley
ROWTON HEATH
1645
N
R. Dee
Hatton Heath
Dodleston
KEY
1 The Cathedral
2 The Castle
3 Bridge Gate
4 Water Gate
5 Bonewaldthorne's Tower
6 Water Tower
7 St. Martin's Gate
8 Morgan's Mount
9 Northgate
10 King Charles's Tower
11 Eastgate
12 Wolfgate
13 Wolf Tower
Beeston Castle
Pulford
Pulford Brook
Rossett
R. Alyn
to Wrexham
Holt
Holt Castle
Farndon
THE SIEGE OF CHESTER 1645
to Nantwich
P.S.W. Beck

Chester

Defender:	(1) Sir Nicholas Byron (R)
	(2) Lord John Byron (R)
Besieger:	Sir William Brereton (P)
Duration:	Intermittently between 18 July 1643 and 3 February 1646
Outcome:	Surrendered on terms

The city of Chester is of great antiquity, originating in the latter half of the first century AD as Deva, the headquarters of the Twentieth Roman Legion. The first defences consisted of a turf wall estimated to have been about 20 feet thick and 16 feet high. As the settlement increased in importance so the wall was rebuilt in stone, with four gates and 26 towers.

The wall, which still exists in its entirety, is two miles in circumference. Its northern and eastern parts follow the line of the Roman defences and contain substantial portions of the original work, but as the city grew in the late twelfth century, the wall had to be extended to the west and south, the towers still being under construction in the fourteenth century.

The Eastgate was the chief entrance and although the original was demolished in 1769, to make way for the increased volume of traffic, an old print exists which shows it as a conventional mediæval gatehouse with two octagonal towers, loopholed, with a chamber above, probably with portcullis and massive gates.

To the north-east in the angle of the walls still stands the semicircular tower known as King Charles's Tower (today a museum) from which, it is said, that unfortunate monarch watched the defeat of his army at the conclusion of the battle of Rowton Heath.

Next is the Northgate, once again obliterated to meet the needs of nineteenth-century traffic; but another drawing comes to our aid showing it to have consisted of two square battlemented towers, with a stepped wall built up to its crest. Proceeding westward, the tower called Morgan's Mount is reached, named for the battery of guns sited here during the Civil War.

The other towers and gates in order of succession are St Martin's

Gate, the Goblin Tower, rebuilt in 1894 on the site of one of the originals, and Bonewaldesthorne's Tower which stands at the north-west angle connected by a wall to the Water Tower which, situated on a lower level, was once surrounded by the river.

Turning southward, one comes to the Watergate, like the others a replacement for the original (built in 1788), once the entrance to the city from the flourishing port that had made Chester both rich and famous, until the silting up of the River Dee interfered seriously with ship traffic, eventually causing its prosperity to be transferred to the heretofore insignificant fishing village called Liverpool. At the most southerly point of the walls where they form an oblique angle are the remains of the castle.

Built by William I in 1070, and rebuilt in stone by Henry III, it consisted of an inner and outer bailey complete with gatehouses and towers. Besides the still extant Agricola's Tower, a heavily-buttressed edifice *c.* twelfth century, old plans show two other square towers in the inner bailey.

Almost at the completion of this description of the city wall – surely the only one in existence that has the rampart walk remaining in a usable state for its entire circumference – the Bridge Gate is reached. The old gate, through which Charles I galloped to escape into Wales after Rowton Heath, led over the Old Dee Bridge and is represented as having two drum towers of a rather lowly appearance, if one may judge by the size of the horse that is also depicted.

Northward is the New Gate, of as recent a date as 1938, which replaced the Wolfe Gate. The latter was counted to be of great antiquity even in the time of the Tudors. Although much was swept away to meet the needs of the practical nineteenth century, Chester still remains a remarkable example of a fortified mediæval city, a time capsule of history.

The Siege

It would seem that, unlike many other towns and cities whose elders preferred to emulate the ostrich, the Mayor and other civic authorities of Chester reacted to the 'warlike and dangerous times' with some vigour even as early as 1640, arranging for men, arms and powder to be available at short notice, putting the city on what can only be called a war footing.

As in other places, the defences had been neglected during the complacent years of peace, their condition being reported to the Council in 1641 as 'the walls in many parts very ruinous, some part fallen down and in other parts reddy to fall into further decay unless it bee speedilie prevented'. The active Council ordered their immediate repair, to be paid for by a special city tax.[1]

In the following year, with the war a reality, the King visited the city on 23 September 1642, doubtless to receive donations to the war chest and encourage the loyal citizens. 'Many noblemen from this and ye neighbouring counties flocked hither with their forces, to the great strengthening of this port.'[2]

Also at this time further efforts were made to put the defences in order. Under the guidance of 'Colonel Ellis, Major Sidney and other skilful engineers who caused . . . a trench to be cut, and mud wall to be made from Deeside without the Barrs to Deeside at the New Tower; the wall to be repaired and lined with earth'.[3] Drawbridges were built at two of the gates, and regarding the Castle 'divers pieces of cannon to be planted in convenient places', continuing with so many other devices and works that either a great deal of money and man hours were expended or the reporter allowed his natural enthusiasm to run away with him.

The first attempt on the defences by Sir William Brereton on Tuesday 18 July 1643 was no more than a probing attack, for after 'pelting the outworks at Boughton with small shot' for two days, he withdrew on the third. The citizens rang the church bells and rejoiced but their rejoicings were somewhat premature, to say the least, for on Tuesday 7 November Brereton, with 'five Cheshire foote companies and three or four troops of horse, and three or four companies of country dragooners, wherewith there joined five companies of Lancashire foote'[4] and an uncertain number of other troops, forced the bridge over the Dee at Farndon, south of the city, despite the fierce resistance of the Royalist garrison of Holt Castle.

Their further progress was reported;[5] 'About six o'clock Thursday evening [9 November] we entered Wrexham, which lyes within 7 miles of Chester, verie commodious to hinder all the passages to Chester.' Nor was this all, for the 'passages neere Chester on the other side att Tarvin and Wirral'[6] were also obstructed.

The circumvallation of the city was being built with precision, for on 11 November Brereton and Sir Thomas Middleton with nine troops of horse and two companies of foot, marched on Hawarden Castle. This was 'a strong castle in very good repair and commodiously situated for blocking up Chester'[7] but it surrendered without a shot fired.

The blockade was already affecting the city, stopping the supplies which the Welsh had been bringing in while the roads were open. In these circumstances it might appear that the days of Chester as a Royalist stronghold were numbered, as indeed they might well have been, but for the fact that a truce with the Irish rebels freed the English Army there for home service.

Landing near Mostyn (Flintshire) on 18 November and in Anglesey in some strength, they were a threat to Brereton's rear that he was quick to recognise, causing him to retreat from Mostyn, Flint and Holywell to Wrexham, afterwards quitting the latter rather precipitately and falling back to Nantwich. The small garrison left in Hawarden Castle held out for more than[8] a fortnight but eventually, despairing of succour, they surrendered on honourable terms.

The Royalist cause was in the ascendant, for in the months following the arrival at Chester of Lord Byron, a nephew of the Governor, with 1000 horse and 300 foot great headway was made against the Parliamentarians, and at Christmas he sallied forth to lay siege to Nantwich. Meeting Brereton between Middlewich and Northwich, Byron drove him from the field, and invested the little town with its defences of mud walls and ditches. On 18 January 1644 an assault was made which was steadfastly repelled.

Sir Thomas Fairfax had been sent to succour the defenders and he came in sight of Nantwich three days later, where he was joined by the remnants of Brereton's troops and battle was joined with the Royalists. After several hours' fierce fighting, during which the issue hung in the balance, the Royalists were dispersed and utterly defeated.

While this was proceeding, Colonel Thomas Mytton had engaged a body of Royalists sent out from Chester to replenish their magazine from Shrewsbury. Meeting them at Ellesmere on 12 January,[9] he had routed them, capturing two very important officers, the Governor of Chester, Sir Nicholas Byron, and Sergeant Major General Sir Richard Willis.

There followed a period of fluctuating fortunes for both sides, hence it was almost a year later that Chester was again under siege. Parliament garrisons were once more sited at Aldford, Hawarden, Trafford, Tarvin and Upton Hall to block supplies reaching the city. Byron attempted to relieve Beeston Castle which was under pressure, but hardly got further than the city gates, for on 27 January 1645 Brereton launched an attack on the Northgate Turnpike. 'The rebels came with scaling ladders to scale the walls, but they had so hot a breakfast as divers went with bullets for concoction – which hindered their drinking ever after',[10] wrote an eyewitness with grim humour.

Once again Chester had a respite, for on 19 February Prince Maurice advanced from Worcester and relieved the city. Further work was done to strengthen the defences, including the demolition of the chapel of St John without the Northgate together with the hospital buildings, to deny cover to the enemy.

The glee of the inhabitants was graphically expressed by the same eyewitness: 'the approach of the Prince frighted so the rebells that they raised the siege and withdrew themselves to the furthest side of Cheshire as remotest from danger'.[11] But their triumph was of short duration for with the departure of Maurice on 13 March, Brereton once again renewed the siege, occupying Eccleston, Dodleston, Pulford 'and as near as Netherlegh'. Lord John Byron, now Governor, wrote to the King's Secretary, complaining of the mismanagement of the King's affairs in Wales.[12] 'I know it is usual for men to exaggerate the importance of those places where their commands lie, but without such self-partiality this case stands unrivalled in relation to his Majesty's affairs.' He complains that the Princes Rupert and Maurice, having used both himself and the city as a convenience, had 'marched away the remainder of the old Irish Regiments . . . to the number of at least 1200, so that I was left in the town with only a garrison of citizens and my own and Colonel Mostin's regiments which both together made not above 600 men'.

He was also obliged to dispense with Mostin's men as they were all proud Welsh gentlemen and not amenable to discipline as a result of which 'the rebels finding the Prince retreated with his army, and the country emptied of all soldiers but such as were necessary for keeping the garrisons returned with all there forces to block up Chester on all sides . . .' Furthermore, in view of the 'considerable army of the enemy, which I am advertised is now advancing towards me' and in spite of the shortage of gun-powder and victual and a desperate need for more 'money for the public service', he would do his best to hold out 'despite the poor means I have left to maintain the place'.

Meanwhile, Sir William Brereton was not without his worries, for he wrote on 21 April,[13] 'Not certain now when the King comes hither . . . they have pressed most of ye horse in these counties and fitted them out for a swifte and quicke march. Report that there first worcke is to relieve Chester . . .' But concerning the eventual capitulation of the city he is more confident. 'Wee are soe neare to Chester on all sides and ye inhabitants therein are much pinched and yet so confident of speedy reliefe . . . If at this tyme they be disappointed in their expectacons . . . the City will before long be surrendered.'

Despite, or because of, his apprehension of a Royalist Army descending upon him from the Midlands, or perhaps another influx of soldiers from Ireland landing in Wales, Brereton pressed the siege with some vigour. On 14 May, he wrote to John Bradshaw 'The siege is drawn up close to Chester and last evening I had intelligence that the people there was in great distress, having little to support them'.

On 17 May, Colonel Duckenfield wrote to Sir William Brereton, 'Besieged in Chester put all their cattel forth to grasse on this side of ye town without interruption. We have not horse enough to keep them in, . . . which may be easily prevented by six troopes of horse . . . Sir Wm. Constable regt. is moving toward our parts soe unless . . . [you] helpe they will ruine us.'

It will be seen by this that the siege was by no means a firm one and required very little to upset all the Parliament plans; indeed all their forces on the Welsh side were shortly withdrawn, although the blockade was continued as vigorously as ever on the English side. This move was occasioned by the march of the King and his 'Oxford Army' northward, which caused a great muster of the Parliament troops at Barlow Moor. One of Brereton's letters states 'have brought up Cheshire horse and dragoons and what foot could possibly be spared . . . and have sent for more'. For the people of Chester, this was the end of the second stage of this prolonged siege.

Although the King's cause was irretrievably ruined at Naseby on 14 June, where he lost his last field army, the siege was not actively resumed until September 1645, despite the pleas of the Committee at Nantwich in August, who wrote to the Speaker regarding 'the great advantage the reducing of the city of Chester would bring to the state and there humble request thereupon'.[14] To this came a stiff reply from Lenthall on 28 August that 'this House defers assistance in reducing Chester . . . hoping affairs may be in a more certain condition with relation to the forces now with the King'. But on 20 September an assault force of 500 horse, 200 dragoons and 700 foot advancing under cover of darkness stormed the suburbs at dawn, seizing a bulwark at Boughton, then the main line of bulwarks on that side, taking the entire suburb up to the Eastgate, and capturing the city sword and mace as trophies. But once again, the affairs of the outside world seemed to be intruding on the siege and preventing its successful conclusion by the Parliament.

For the King with an army of about 4000 men, mostly survivors of Marston Moor and Naseby, was coming to Chester's aid.

Messengers were sent post haste by the Committee of Both Kingdoms to Colonel General Sydenham Poyntz, who was endeavouring to intercept the King and who had missed him at Worcester, stating 'we have information that the King with most of his forces is moving towards Chester. If he be not followed our forces that have lately so happily suppressed the suburbs and are in a fair way to take the town will be endangered.'

The besiegers pursued their task with even this threat hanging over them. On 22 September 'the east side of our walls near to the new gate receive a visit from their artillerie . . . thirty two shots were made and by them a breach at which ten men abreast may enter',[15] writes a Royalist eyewitness. Obviously the Parliament gunners were making good use of the short range afforded by the captured suburb.

After a forced march, the King and his army reached Chester, which he entered with about a third of his force under Lord Astley, Lord Charles Gerrard and the Earl of Lichfield (Bernard Stuart), while the remainder, all cavalry to the number of about 3000 commanded by Sir Marmaduke Langdale, crossed the River Dee by a bridge of boats, eight miles below the city, designing to fall upon the besiegers from the rear.

Determined not to miss the chance of engaging the Royalists, Poyntz reached Chester by a night march, arriving in the early hours of 24 September. He achieved no surprise, however, for through an intercepted letter Langdale knew of his approach and promptly charged and drove him back with loss. But the Parliament horse were not broken. A strange stalemate ensued. Langdale could not retire on Chester with Poyntz in his rear, and similarly Poyntz could not join the besiegers while Langdale barred the way. The first side to obtain reinforcements was assured of victory. Langdale seems to have been dilatory about this. Not so his opponent who promptly got in touch with the besiegers and equally promptly was aided. Somewhere about midday 500 horse under Colonel Michael Jones and 300 foot under Adjutant General James Lothian marched round the Royalist flank and joined themselves to Poyntz who was drawn up on Hatton Heath two miles to the south of Rowton.

Throughout the morning the citizens had been working to clear away the material with which they had barricaded the Eastgate, in preparation for a sally, but it was not until 3 p.m. that the King ordered it.

Meanwhile,[16] Langdale was being attacked flank and front by the Parliament force and, after a brief struggle, the outnumbered Royalists broke and fled. By this time, the gateway cleared, Gerrard and Lichfield emerged and formed up under the walls, where they were attacked by the remainder of the besieging force. When Langdale's survivors arrived on the scene, followed by the pursuing Roundheads, both sides became inextricably mixed in a terrible melée. With the lack of distinctive uniforms, none could tell friend from foe. To make matters worse, the garrison fired indiscriminately into the packed mass from the walls. With what agony of mind must the King have contemplated the slaughter from his viewpoint on the Phoenix Tower on the north-east corner of the city wall, and later from the Cathedral Tower. The loss to him was overwhelming, at this stage of the war, with 600 killed and 800 Royalists captured.

After this disaster the King lost no time in quitting the city, ordering the Mayor to make the best terms he could if no relief arrived in 10 days. Despite some heartening promises from the King via Lord Digby, there was no doubt that Chester was now in the lion's mouth.

On 26 September a summons to surrender was sent and rejected. The story of the siege from this point onward is one of determined resistance on the one side under starvation conditions, and equally determined and patient assault on the other. The Parliament guns thundered ceaselessly, creating breaches which were quickly blocked with earth and rubble. Mines were met with counter-mines. On 8–9 October letters were exchanged between the commanders, to no avail.

A network of trenches was to be constructed round Chester but the work was held up for 'lack of pyoneers'. On 9 November Brereton reported 'the city is closely blockaded on the Cheshire side there being posts at Pulford, Bretton, Doddleston, Eccleston and Brewers Hall. The guards are kept close to the walls and we have cast and made such defences and breastworks against their gates and sally ports as there is no great danger of them issuing out to among us.'

At last there was some good news for the besiegers. Beeston Castle, which had been beleaguered for a year, surrendered on 16 November. A parley was made three days later but Byron proved as obdurate as ever and followed it up with an impudent sally of 80 horse upon the guard on the Welsh side. It was only a feint to draw the watchers' attention away from the two boats laden with gunpowder and combustibles which they hoped would drift with the tide and so destroy the bridge of boats. On 28 November Brereton wrote to the Speaker 'the besieged in Chester remain very obstinate and do not seem inclinable to embrace any overtures made for their preservation'.[17]

The siege chronicle is full of the terrors of the constant sniping and bombardment by the besiegers: 'Lieutenant Morgell is slain upon his guard.' 'Mr Richardson the Sheriff is likewise shot dead.' 'Levi Dodd is slain through a loophole.' 'Captain Ffoulkes is slain', and so the dreary catalogue goes on. The Parliament troops had now brought up a mortar which 'grinds our dwellings to dust and ashes', and on 10 December, 'eleven huge grenadoes like so many demy-phaetons threaten to set the city, if not the world on fire. This was a terrible night indeed.'

By 30 December the city was completely surrounded and on 7 January 1646 Brereton, having intelligence that many of the poor had died from starvation in the city, again sent in a surrender summons, which was ignored. Another was sent and another. On 15 January, Brereton received a letter signed by Charles Walley, the Mayor, which made it plain that they had persuaded Byron that no useful purpose was served by holding out longer.

The time that elapsed between the receipt of this letter and the actual occupation of the city on 3 February was taken up with negotiations over terms, until an acceptable basis was found. When the Parliament troops entered they 'beholde and mark the ruins of . . . the moste enchante and famous cittie of Chester . . . the particular demolitions of it, now most grevious to the spectators and more woeful to the inhabitants thereof'.[18]

REFERENCES

1 *Assembly Book*, Vol. 2, Chester Corporation MSS No. 527
2 Harleian MS.2155
3 *Ibid*
4 Brereton's letter to Speaker Lenthal, 11 November 1643, in *Sir William Brereton's Letter Books*, Add. MSS 11331–11333
5 *Ibid*
6 Brereton to Speaker, 15 November, Portland MSS.153
7 See Rushworth, *Historical Collections* . . . Vol. 2, part 3, pp. 298–301

[8] A list of prisoners may be found in a letter from Sir Thomas Fairfax to the Earl of Essex dated 25 January 1644 in Rushworth, Vol. 2, part 3, p. 302

[9] 'A true realtion of a notable surprise &c. at Ellesmere'

[10] Harleian MS.2125

[11] *Ibid*

[12] 26 April 1645, John, Lord Byron to George, Lord Digby Principal Secretary, C.S.P.D.

[13] Sir William Brereton to the Committee of Both Kingdoms, Add. MSS. 11331, folio 5

[14] 23 September 1645, Sir Thomas Widrington to Sir Henry Vane, senior, C.S.P.D.

[15] Harleian MS.2125

[16] Many eyewitness accounts of Rowton Heath exist. The most exhaustive is that of the 'Chaplain to our Forces' to be found in *Cheshire Civil War Tracts* 28, Chetham Society Publications. See also Burne and Young, *The Great Civil War*, 1959

[17] Additional MSS.11332

[18] *Cheshire Sheaf*, 3rd Series

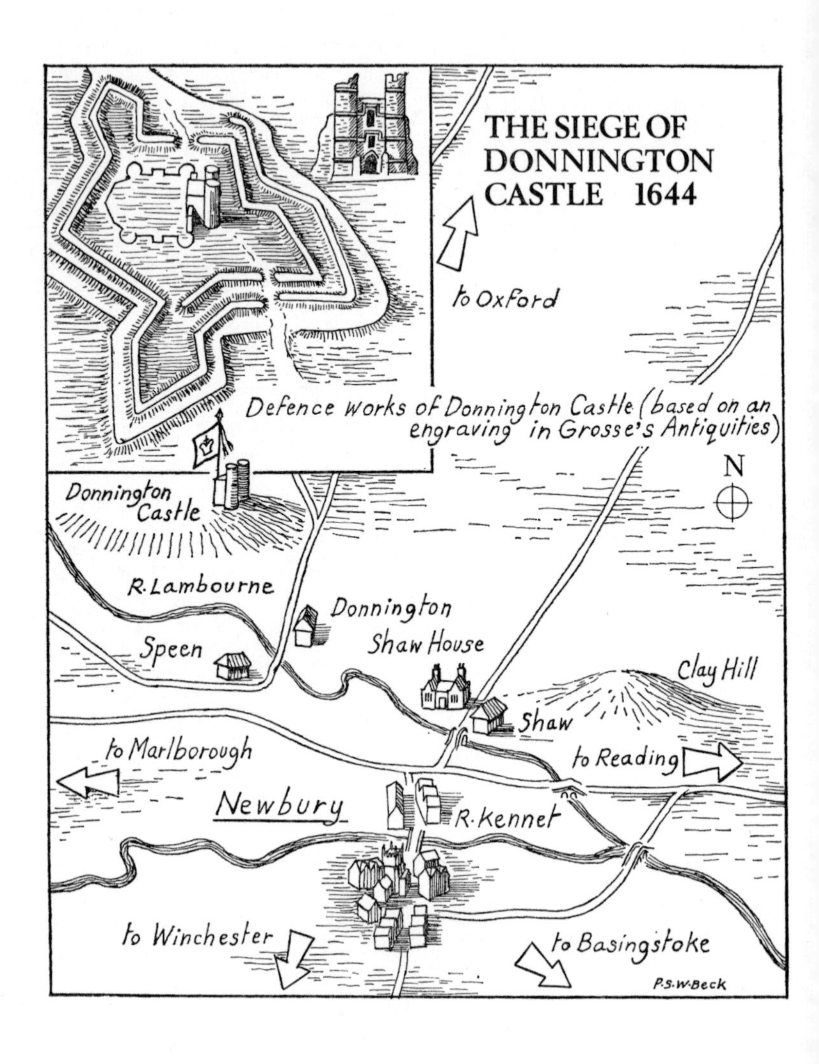
THE SIEGE OF
DONNINGTON
CASTLE 1644
to Oxford
Defence works of Donnington Castle (based on an
engraving in Grosse's Antiquities)
N
Donnington
Castle
R. Lambourne
Donnington
Speen
Shaw House
Clay Hill
Shaw
to Marlborough
to Reading
Newbury
R. Kennet
to Winchester
to Basingstoke
P.S.W. Beck

Donnington Castle

Defender:	Colonel (Sir) John Boys (R)
Besieger:	(1) Lieutenant General John Middleton (P) 31 July 1644 (2) Colonel Jeremy Horton, 29 September 1644 (3) Earl of Manchester and Sir William Waller October 1644 (4) Colonel John Dalbier, November 1645–April 1646
Duration:	Collectively one year and nine months
Outcome:	Surrendered on terms 1 April 1646

The castle is situated on a spur of high ground 400 feet above sea level and commands the east to west road, commonly known as the Great Bath Road, and the equally important route from Southampton to Oxford and the North. The modern aspect to the south discloses wide views over a well-wooded landscape towards Highclere, while to the east a large stand of trees comes right up to the site, partially obscuring the vista of rural landscape. In the fourteenth century, the manor of Donnington belonged to the family of Abberbury, and it was the last male of that house, Sir Richard, who built the castle on this knoll above the River Lambourne, having obtained his 'license to crenellate' in 1385. 'Know that by our special grace we have given license . . . to our beloved and faithful Richard Abberbury the elder, that he may build anew and fortify with stone and lime and crenellate a castle on his own land at Donnington, Berks . . .'[1]

To him is attributable the three-storey gatehouse whose flint walls stand 65 feet tall which is all that remains intact today. This, with two drum towers rising high at the outer angles, did duty as keep. It is banded with five stone courses, the upper ones being decorated with gargoyle type heads. The entrance is barred on both sides by latticed iron gates, through which the vaulted ceiling can be seen to have a leaf-type pattern in the bays. Extending from the gateway are two broken walls that have the appearance of being part of an outwork. It might seem that the builders of Donnington had an eye for comfort as well as military necessities for the bailey or courtyard, which is about 110 feet by 69 feet internally, was lined with ranges of apartments on all sides and was described by Camden in 1586 as 'having a fair prospect on all sides and windows in all sides very lightsome'.[2]

The outer plan can still be traced by the remains of the flint walls which are nowhere above three feet high. The gatehouse projects forward from the east front for its whole length. The courtyard, which was cobbled, was oblong with a bowed end to the west. At each corner was a small round tower of no particular substance, probably serving no more useful purpose than to contain a staircase for access to the ramparts. The northern and southern faces were broken by square towers,[3] the southern tower being of greater strength than the other. It is thought that these towers would have been almost as high as the existing towers of the gatehouse when complete.[4]

The line of the earthworks which Sir John Boys had constructed during the Civil War when he held the castle for the King may still be plainly seen. Grose's plan of the work (1773) shows the great bastions shaped like a spear head or abbreviated diamond that housed cannons to the east, south and north-west. On the vulnerable north and east fronts, the earthworks formed a double line. It might be reasonable to suppose that these fortifications were made in the time-honoured fashion used in the Iron Age and employed by everyone in need of hasty fortifications ever since. A wide deep ditch is dug and the earth from it thrown inwards to form a wall which is revetted by wood or stone. The defences at Oxford were made in this way with 'many strong bulwarks so strongly flanking one another that nothing could be more exactly done . . . on the outside of the ditch it was strongly palisaded and without that again were digged several pits in the ground so that a single foeman could not without difficulty approach the brink of the ditch'.[5] Often pointed stakes were set at an angle in the ditch itself as an added deterrent.

We are told that, bearing in mind that to the north-east the castle was on a level with Snelsmore Common and hence was more open to attacks, Boys made a fortification with a trench and palisade 'the top made of great thicknesse and stronge as covered over with bricks and earth proped with greate beames and layed over with packes of wall [wool] to prevent the execution of Mortor grenades'.[6] The cost of these defences was formidable, somewhere in the region of £1000, which was raised by a weekly contribution levied on the citizens of Newbury and the inhabitants of the hundreds of Kintbury-Eagle, Compton and Faircross.[7] The defenders must have thought the money well spent for without them it would have been impractical to have held out so long, with the castle itself making such an excellent target.

The Siege

Surely Mr John Packer must be accounted one of the most unfortunate landowners of the Civil War, for in 1640 or thereabouts, he became the owner of Donnington Castle. No doubt it added to his prestige as a Member of Parliament to have such a country seat, but as he was of Puritan sympathies he soon lost it to the Royalist forces who garrisoned and held it for the duration of the war. Packer's friends had perforce to knock it down and when it was returned to him in 1647, it was so ruinous that he resigned himself to living in a town house for the short remainder of his life. Basing House and Donnington have much in common for both commanded a vital trade road.

Shortly after the first battle of Newbury, the King ordered Colonel John Boys to garrison the castle in order to command the great western road with a force of about 200 foot,[8] 25 horse and four pieces of cannon. Towards the end of July 1644 the Parliament's chief commander, the Earl of Essex, detached Lieutenant General John Middleton with between 3000 and 4000 horse and dragoons to reduce the stronghold. Deploying his forces he sent a summons couched in these terms to Boys:[9] 'Sir, I demand you to render me Donnington Castle for the use of the King and Parliament. If you please to entertain a present treaty you shall have honourable terms. My desire to spare blood makes me propose this. I desire your answer. John Middleton.'

If he expected to intimidate the Royalist commander by numbers he had mistaken his man, for back came the resolute answer, 'Sir, I am instructed by his Majesty's express commands and I have not yet learned to obey any other Sovereign. To spare blood, do as you please, but myself and those that are with me are fully resolved to venture ourselves in maintaining what we are entrusted with, which is the answer of John Boys, Donnington Castle, July 31 1644.' Lacking siege artillery, Middleton tried to take the place by assault, his men rushing forward with scaling ladders only to be driven back with heavy losses. After his repulse he pressed matters no further, having orders to join Essex in the west, but this did not mean that Donnington was to be left alone.

Colonel Jeremy Horton, Adjutant General to Major General Brown and Governor of Abingdon, took over the task and decided to lay siege to the castle instead of attempting the costly business of another assault. He raised a battery 'at the foot of the hill toward Newbury'. For 12 days he bombarded the stronghold, shattering three of the southern towers and a portion of the wall. Thinking the morale of the garrison must be now at a low ebb, he sent a threatening letter demanding surrender, pointing out that he had been reinforced and offering quarter, making a deadline of[10] 'Wednesday the next at 10 of the clock in the forenoon, and further we testify (in the presence of God) that if this our favour be not accepted . . . there shall be no active man amongst you have his life . . .' Back came the mocking answer from Boys. 'Sir, neither your new addition of forces or your high threatening language shall deter me or the honest men with me from our loyalty to our Sovereign . . . and for the matter of quarter yours may expect the like on Wednesday, or sooner if you please . . .'

On Friday 4 October the Earl of Manchester himself took charge of the siege and determined to settle the matter once and for all by a general assault. But the men[11] 'being well informed of the resolution of those within declined that hot service and plied it with their artillery'. After 19 days, hearing of the approach of the King's army, they withdrew. On 22 October 1644 Charles knighted Colonel John Boys for his service on Red Heath (said by some to be Wash Common). The second battle of Newbury followed five days later and Donnington was a key point. The King's position was triangular with one corner resting on Shaw House, one on the village of Speen and the third on Donnington. The Parliamentarians had an excellent chance to crush the King irreparably, for they outnumbered him two to one, but the opportunity was lost through lack of co-operation between their three armies due to the professional jealousy of the commanders. Musketry continued on into the night with Boys firing his cannon into the enemy as occasion presented itself. The King made his escape with his Life-guard, leaving his treasure, the crown, great seal and cannon, in the safe keeping of Boys at Donnington. Next day Sir William Waller drew his entire army round the castle. Once again Boys was summoned to surrender. Once again he refused with spirit. It seems that he was only saved on this occasion by the dissensions of the Parliament commanders and by the death of the officer in charge of the assault.

On 8 November, the King, having been joined by Rupert, sent a party of six or seven thousand horse and foot to relieve Donnington Castle and[12] 'to fetch away things out of the Castle as were most material . . .' By 10 November, this somewhat daring mission had been accomplished, and all the goods left after the battle taken away, with the exception of a number of the heavier, more cumbersome guns that were left behind for the use of the garrison. During the first half of 1645 Parliament had more weighty matters to attend to than Boys, but the garrison with its constant raids and sallies was a festering sore in the side of the Roundheads and when the war was virtually won they turned to reducing the garrisons which still held out for the King.

After Cromwell and Dalbier had crushed Basing House on 14 November 1645, the latter was detached to deal with Donnington, where Boys, with four of his towers down, held on with bulldog-like tenacity. Hearing of his coming the Royalists fired the village of Donnington and other local villages to deny accommodation to the Roundheads.[13] 'Dulbere being thus prevented of his quarters at Donnington towne which was within a halfe mile of the Castle and also of other Ajatiente villages and houwses, loges his partre of foote in Newbury and quarters his horsse in the Ajatiente villages so that Donnington Castell may be said to be now blocked but not besieged.' And there they stayed through all the bitter winter months; but with the advent of spring Dalbier took the field and commenced firing on the castle with a heavy mortar, which caused such devastation within the already shot-riddled fortress that many of the garrison ran out into the earthworks to avoid the crashing masonry.[14]

Even Boys seemed to realise that the writing was on the wall, for he held a parley with Dalbier, the result of which was the granting of passes to Oxford to two officers (Captains Osborne and Donne) to gain the King's orders. When they arrived, Charles's instructions were definite:[15] 'Hee shoulde gette the beste conditions that he could for himselfe and his, and yet if possibly he could he shoulde marche off to Oxford and bringe of all the Artillery of the Castell with hime.'

And so it was that Sir John Boys made honourable terms with Colonel John Dalbier that allowed him and his garrison[16] to march out with their colours flying, drums beating, their matches lighted, bullets in their mouths and bandoliers filled with powder. After they had marched out on 1 April 1646 the castle was sacked and all the lead stolen to the great discomforture of its Roundhead owner.

REFERENCES

[1] 9 R II Patent Rolls
[2] Wood, *Donnington Castle*, HMSO, p. 15
[3] *Ibid*, p. 17
[4] *Ibid*, p. 20
[5] Report of Fairfax Council of War, 3 May 1646
[6] *Capt. Knight's relation*, Clarendon State Papers 2062, Bodleian
[7] Richard Symonds, *Diary of the Marches of the Royal Army during the Civil War*, p. 144
[8] *Ibid*
[9] *True Informer*, 1 August–17 August 1644
[10] See Money, *The first and second battles of Newbury and the siege of Donnington Castle*, 1881, p. 147
[11] Clarendon
[12] *Perfect Passages*, 6 November 1644
[13] *Knight*
[14] *Moderate Intelligencer*, 31 March 1646
[15] *Knight*
[16] Surrender terms in *Perfect Occurences*, 27 March–3 April 1646

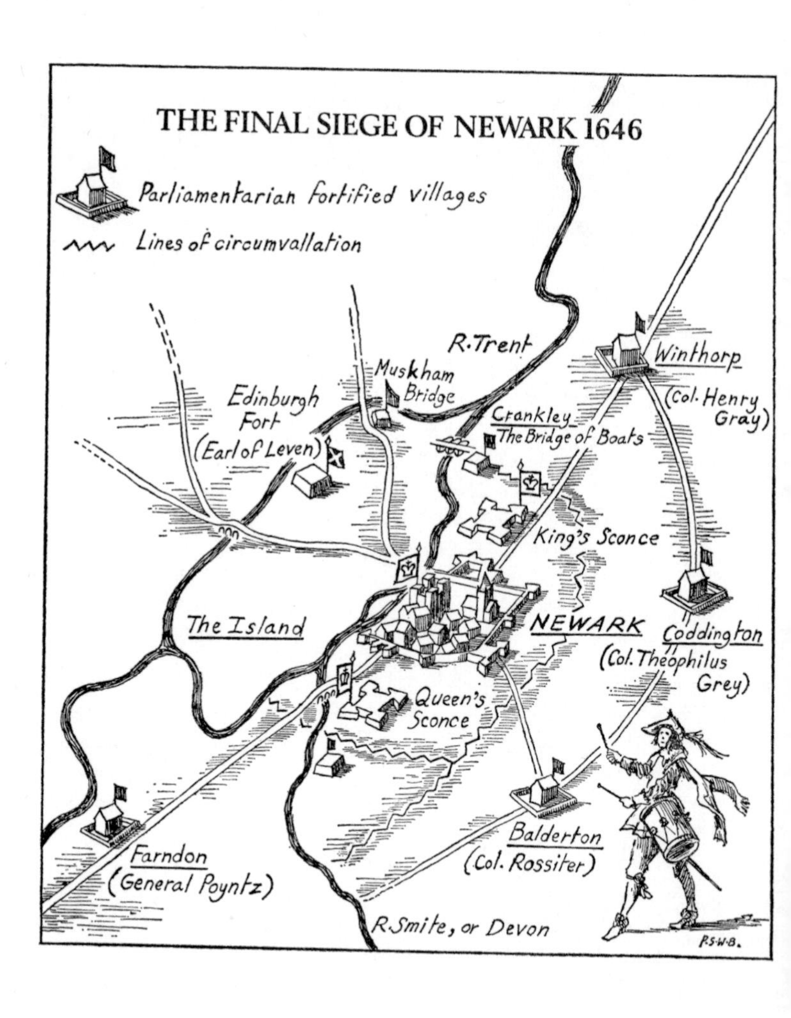
THE FINAL SIEGE OF NEWARK 1646
Parliamentarian fortified villages
Lines of circumvallation
R. Trent
Muskham Bridge
Edinburgh Fort (Earl of Leven)
Crankley
The Bridge of Boats
Winthorp (Col. Henry Gray)
King's Sconce
The Island
NEWARK
Coddington (Col. Theophilus Grey)
Queen's Sconce
Farndon (General Poyntz)
Balderton (Col. Rossiter)
R. Smite, or Devon
P.S.W.B.

Newark

Defenders:	(1) Sir John Henderson (R)
	(2) Sir Richard Byron (R)
	(3) Lord John Belasyse (R)
Besiegers:	(1) Major General Thomas Ballard (P)
	(2) Sir John Meldrum (P)
	(3) Alexander Leslie, Earl of Leven (S)
	Colonel General Sydenham Poyntz (P)
Duration:	(1) 27–9 February 1643
	(2) 29 February–21 March 1644
	(3) 26 November 1645–8 May 1646
Outcome:	(1) Attackers repulsed
	(2) Relieved by Prince Rupert
	(3) Surrendered by order of the King

A glance at the geographical location of Newark will show that it is this factor and not its commercial importance or size that made it valuable strategically. The Roman Fosse Way bisects it from south-west to north-east, connecting the Royal headquarters at Oxford to Lincoln and other places vital to the Royalists. At Newark too the Great North Road crossed the River Trent north-west to south-east, linking important points like Pontefract and York to Stamford and, eventually, London.

There is evidence that the town was sufficiently important to have been made defensible in the pre-Conquest period – the Saxon name for it was Niweweorce – but it was not until the early part of the twelfth century that the Bishop of Lincoln caused the Trent to be bridged and a castle to be erected to command the passage. By 1129 it was described as a magnificent castle of ornate construction,[1] but due to the ravages of the Civil War only the gatehouse and the west tower remain.

Despite royal patronage in the thirteenth century, Newark never seemed to achieve the growth or the eminence of York or Lincoln, and certainly the citizens seem to have had little faith in its future, for the area enclosed by the mediæval town walls was very modest, not exceeding 30 acres.[2] Starting at the western side of the castle the defences ran south-easterly across Bar Gate following Slaughterhouse Lane and Mount Lane, turning right along the south-western edge of the churchyard and proceeding as far as Lombard Street, turning right again and following this road to the river once more.

There would seem to have been gates at the junction of Bar Gate and North Gate (North Bar), South Gate at the meeting of Mill Gate and Castle Gate, East Gate in Bridge Street and very probably another giving access to Trent Bridge. All that remains of these ancient fortifications are a few scattered fragments, the largest of which are situated on the corner of Lombard Street and Castle Gate.

By 1642 these defences were quite useless, being masked by the expansion of the town that had extruded through them compactly to the south-west, while narrow fingers of development had spread out along the Fosse Way – appropriately called ribbon development in today's terminology – in both directions. Between the north-west boundary and the river was the Spittal, a fine house built on the site of the mediæval hospital of St Leonard by the Countess of Exeter at a cost of £2000. This was due to play a significant part in the forthcoming action.

North-west of the town was and is the Island,[3] a large flat area approximately one mile by two miles, formed by the bifurcation of the Trent a mile above the town and its reunion a mile below. It was overlooked by the guns of the castle. Three smaller islands lay in the town branch of the Trent. They are important to this narrative only because one of them served as a stepping stone in the construction of a boat bridge during Sir John Meldrum's siege.

A ring of villages and manor houses are strategically sited round the town just as though they had been planned for the convenience of besiegers, from two to 13 miles distant. Even more useful were the roads which connected them to Newark and to one another. Of these villages Winthorpe, Coddington, Balderton and Farndon were to be fortified and others used for quartering soldiers in the coming conflict.

It is not to be supposed that the Parliamentarians had a monopoly of military awareness. Like an astute chess player stationing pawns the Royalists were to use Norwell House (six miles north of Newark), Wiverton Hall (12 miles south-west), Belvoir Castle (13 miles south), Shelford Manor (10 miles south-west) and Thurgarston Priory (seven miles west) as outposts.

The Siege

As has been shown, the town was hardly in a condition to be defended in 1642 when the Civil War commenced. The only usable part of the mediæval defences was the castle which formed a valuable strongpoint. In the latter part of the year, Sir John Henderson, a Scots professional soldier with continental experience, was made Governor of Newark, and immediately commenced work on defence positions. We are told[4] that the extent of them was 'only round the town and leaving out Mill Gate and North Gate with the Earl of Exeter's house'. Apparently their construction was hasty and somewhat sketchy for the same source states 'they were very low and thin, and with a dry ditch which most men might easily leap over'.

The first attempt to take the town was more in the nature of an assault than a siege. Henderson seems to have been a lively, vigorous officer who obviously believed in the old maxim 'the best form of defence is attack', for upon learning that Major General Thomas Ballard intended to attempt Newark late in February 1643, he led out 10 troops of cavalry, marching at night to Beckingham hoping to take the Parliamentarians by surprise. But Ballard's scouts had warned him of the Royalist's approach, and, finding that he was expected, Henderson prudently withdrew. The Roundhead advance seems to have been tardy if we believe Lucy Hutchinson who speaks of the 'slowth and untoward carriage of Ballard'.[5]

The forces of Nottingham, Derby and Lincoln totalling about 6000 men and 10 sakers arrived at Newark on 27 February. The Royalists occupied Beacon Hill to hinder them, but, finding this pointless without ordnance, fell back on the town.

Next day, Ballard summoned Newark to surrender 'to King and Parliament' and, being refused, divided his command into three parts, one of which occupied the smouldering ruins of the Spittal which had been torched by Henderson's order to avoid just this contingency, while his ordnance fired 80 shots into the town.

After this initial 'softening up' cannonade, a general assault was planned. Northward the Lincolnshire troops moved out from the Spittal and drove the Royalists from their works and, according to one account,[6] fought their way up to the Cross where they were caught in a cross-fire from musketeers and cannon stationed in barns and outbuildings against such an emergency. The southern assault made less headway but had taken a ditch within a pistol shot of the works.

From here they kept up a running fire of musketry for several hours.

Eventually, all the Parliament forces were concentrated in one sector, hoping apparently that their combined weight might force an entry. At about 3 p.m. they stormed, but their preparations had been 'perceived by the wary Gouvenour' who strengthened the defence in their quarters and 'entertained them with a hotter service than they expected'. After three fruitless hours Ballard's men 'began to wax weary of the worke'.[7]

Observing this, Henderson counter-attacked and drove the Roundheads back pell-mell to the safety of their horse, over-running three of their guns. Mrs Hutchinson's view of the matter is that Ballard was motivated by regard to 'preserve his olde patrons'[8] in the city, and hence hindered the attack as much as he could without 'betraying his friendes', and was deaf to the entreaties of the 'lieftenante-collonell [who] in vaine importuned Ballard to send them ammunition and reliefe, but could obteine neithere and so they were forc'd unwillingly, to retreate'.

The next day 'all the captaines importun'd Ballard that they might fall on againe, but he would neither consent nor give any reason for his denial so that the Nottingham forces return'd with greate dissatisfaction'.

On 11 October 1643 occurred 'the action at Winceby'. Hardly of the proportions to be called a battle, the Royalists – who had been ordered by Newcastle to aid Bolingbroke Castle now threatened by Manchester – consisted of 1500–2000 horse and 800 dragoons commanded by Henderson, and drawn from the garrisons of Newark, Lincoln and Gainsborough; while the Parliamentarians under Manchester, with Cromwell and Sir Thomas Fairfax as subordinates, numbered at least 1500 horse and 6000 foot.

The outcome was a total victory for the Roundheads[9] with their opponents dispersed over a wide area with considerable casualties. The advantage thus gained led to the re-conquest of Lincolnshire, Gainsborough falling to Gell on 20 December as Lincoln itself had a month previously, leaving Newark dangerously isolated. But apart from denuding the countryside of cattle and sheep, with a view to causing the garrison to consume their supplies with the consequent risk of shortages, they were not as yet in a position to beleaguer the town. Henderson's reputation may well have been tarnished by Winceby, for he was shortly replaced by Sir Richard Byron.

The first siege commenced on 29 March 1644, when Sir John

Meldrum (who had succeeded Ballard), with a large force consisting of some 2000 horse, 5000 foot and 13 pieces of ordnance, arrived at Newark.[10] On 6 March he won control of the Island, storming Muskham Bridge and destroying Gervase Holles's regiment. Having built a bridge of boats to make easy access with his headquarters at the Spittal, he totally invested the town. An effort to relieve the garrison at this time totalling 2000 men, by Colonel Gervase Lucas, Governor of Belvoir Castle, was repulsed a few days later,[11] but at the same time an assault by Meldrum on 8 March was beaten off by the garrison.

Succour was, however, at hand. Prince Rupert received direct orders on 12 March while he was visiting Chester to go to the aid of the 'vital fortress of Newark'. The Prince was suffering from a great shortage of troops, but such a thing had never deterred him before and did not now. Messengers were sent far and wide ordering garrisons to disgorge men, and in many cases to commanders to present themselves personally. Major Will Legge was sent on ahead to collect as many musketeers as could be spared from the Irish regiments garrisoning Shrewsbury. Tillier embarked 1120 men in boats and descended the Severn to Bridgnorth where he joined Rupert with about 800 horse on 15 March. They then proceeded towards Ashby-de-la-Zouch where Lord Loughborough had concentrated 2700 men. Meldrum does not seem to have been unaware of these preparations, but rather to have been somewhat over-confident in the strength of his position and numbers. The Royalists reached Lichfield on 17 March via Chirk, Shrewsbury and Bridgnorth. Meldrum attempted to interpose his horse in the path of Sir Edward Hartop's force to prevent a juncture with Loughborough, but failed miserably in this aim, with disastrous effect. Rupert joined his forces at Ashby on 18 March, was at Rempstone on the following day and Bingham on 20 March.

A battle was now inevitable. Advancing in the early hours of the 21st, Rupert occupied Beacon Hill from where he could see the Parliamentary force drawn up in line of battle. The foot were lined up about the Spittal with the horse in four great bodies on the lower slopes of the hill. The left wing of the horse was under Colonel Edward Rossiter while Colonel Francis Thornhagh commanded the right.[12]

The action commenced about 9 a.m., Rossiter charging the right-hand Royalist squadron and driving them back up the hill on to their reserve. The intervention of a troop under Captain Clement Martin turned the tide and the Roundheads were beaten off after bitter fighting. On the opposite wing, the Lincolnshire horse had fled at the outset, leaving the Nottinghamshire men to fight as best they might and eventually the entire Roundhead horse were driven back on the Spittal, Thornhagh's wing pell-mell,[13] Rossiter's in good order.

By this time, the Royalist foot came up and invested Meldrum's position, Tillier to the north-east, Newark itself to the south-west and Rupert to the south-east. Part of the garrison was sent on to the Island to cut Meldrum's communications between the fort at Muskham Bridge and the Spittal.

The tables were now turned, for the besiegers were now the besieged. The factious Roundhead commanders with their jealous quarrels, together with the mutiny of the Norfolk Redcoats, made Meldrum's position untenable and he sounded a parley; the outcome of which was that he was allowed to march away with his drums, colours, horses, swords and baggage, but all his guns, firearms and ammunition had to be left for the victor. It was a bitter loss for the Roundhead cause, for Rupert obtained 3000 muskets and 11 brass guns, including the famous 32-pounder, four yards long, from Hull, named 'Sweet Lips' after a well-known local whore.[14]

This quick and clean-cut victory extended the life of the town for another two years,[15] the Parliamentarians losing 200 men, the Royalist less than half that number.

In the months that followed, great events stirred on the national scene, all of which had an effect, some direct, some indirect, on the garrison at Newark.

In the south, Cheriton was fought and lost by the Royalists causing 'His Majesty to wage a defensive rather than an offensive war'.[16] Newark contributed to the army that fought at the disastrous battle of Marston Moor when the North was lost to the King permanently, at least four regiments of horse being absent from the garrison – Dallison's, Eyre's, Pelham's and Tuke's. Records speak of various forays and sallies during the remainder of 1644, one of which was so discreditable, with the Royalist losses greater than they could really afford, that it may well have caused the replacement of Sir Richard Byron as Governor by Sir Richard Willys about January 1645.

The King's cause was virtually ruined by the defeat at Naseby, the final major battle of the Great Civil War on 14 June 1645. Now the northern and midland garrisons still loyal to the King could virtually be reduced at leisure.

It was not until 26 November 1645 that the final siege of Newark began with the appearance of the Earl of Leven and the Scots Army.

Like Meldrum he possessed himself of Muskham Bridge soon after his arrival.

Colonel General Sydenham Poyntz and Colonel Edward Rossiter moved to join him during the first weeks of December, quartering their men around Long Bennington and Claypole. The Nottinghamshire and Derbyshire forces were at Farndon while the Lincoln foot were at Beckingham.

Due to the quarrel between the King and Rupert after the fall of Bristol any person that was known to be pro-Rupert was in disfavour. It did not help Willys at all that he had signed Rupert's petition to the King and had even voiced his complaints in person. It was the logical outcome of his loyalty to the Prince, therefore, that he had been replaced as Governor of Newark by Lord John Belasyse who commanded the garrison for the remainder of its occupation by the Royalists. Internal politics apart, he was an excellent choice, remodelling the garrison and revictualling the town for the siege he knew to be imminent. The improved defences he caused to be constructed were composed of[17] 'strong bastions, earthworks, half moons, counterscarps, redoubts, pitfalls, and an impregnable line of earth and turf, palisaded and stockaded and every part so furnished with great guns and cannon that this bulky bulwark of Newark represented to the besiegers one complete sconce'.

Most of the artillery left behind by Meldrum was disposed around these defences, including the great gun 'Sweet Lips'. After the Meldrum siege, the Spittal, which had proved to be too useful to the enemy even in ruins, was demolished:[18] 'before the third [siege] there was not one stone left unthrown down'. In its place was built a great detached fort with bastions called the King's Sconce. On the opposite side of town, that is to the south-west, there was another similar fort covering three acres commanding a view over the meadows which was named, appropriately enough, the Queen's Sconce, which is still in existence.[19] Its companion was destroyed late in the nineteenth century, and of the town enceinte only slight and fragmentary remains survive.

In the majority of the villages occupied in the last sieges there are traces of the earthworks thrown up by the besiegers, most consisting of a few eroded banks or ditches. These were, of course, too far from the town to effectively block it off from access to the surrounding countryside, so the besiegers laboured without respite on the construction of two lines of circumvallation to enclose the town and seal it off from the outside world. This work, consisted of a chain of small earthwork forts, the largest being named for the commanders in that sector (e.g. Rossiter's, Craford's and Gray's Sconce) linked together by a rampart and trench. Of this tremendous project which was commenced in February and completed by 21 March,[20] stretching from Crankley Point to the River Devon, little now remains, although aerial photos reveal more. On the Island the Scots were busy too, building as a headquarters the great fortified camp they nostalgically called Edinburgh.

The arrival of Scottish, Yorkshire and Eastern Association reinforcements brought the numbers of the blockading army to round about 16000 enabling them to effectively tighten their grip. This did not prevent the garrison issuing out in some strength to probe the besiegers' works.

In February and again, more successfully, in March they attacked the fort at Muskham Bridge[21] – the eroded remains of which still exist – and on the latter occasion were only driven back with difficulty. To combat further excursions of this sort two boat bridges were built, one at Muskham and one at Crankley Point, which latter was defended by a new, strong fort.

But a more powerful ally than cannon or sword was abroad in the town – the plague. According to Lucy Hutchinson it 'was so raging there it nearly desolated the place'.[22] On 28 March Belasyse was called upon to surrender, and he temporised by asking that he might send a messenger to the King for orders, a request that, not unnaturally, was refused.

Poyntz had been busily engaged on damming the Rivers Trent and Smite aiming to divert their courses away from the town, an endeavour in which he succeeded by mid-April. The besiegers were gradually closing in and by the end of the month were within carbine shot of defences. On the Island the Scots had taken a work called Sandhills Sconce[23] from which they could mount ordnance to bombard the castle.

On 27 April Belasyse sued for terms and his commissioners met those of the besiegers on 2 May. Charles had by now become a prisoner of the Scots and sent an order to Belasyse to surrender the town, which he did on 6 May 'on prettie handsome termes, but much discontented that the King should have no more regard to them who had bene so constant to his service'.[24]

According to Thornton, the townsfolk and garrison had no wish to give up the struggle. The Mayor, one Smith,[25] begged the Governor to sally forth and cut his way out rather than yield. Whatever Belasyse felt – and he wept at the surrender – there was no gainsaying the King's command, and on 8 May he marched out with the remainder of the depleted garrison.

REFERENCES

1 Henry of Huntingdon, p. 266
2 See *Newark-on-Trent – The Civil War Siege Works*, 1964, Royal Commission on Historical Monuments, p. 28 based on siege plan
3 *Ibid*, p. 26
4 See Twentyman, MS. account of Siege of Newark in Brown, *History of Newark*, 1907, Vol. II, p. 59
5 Hutchinson, *Memoirs* of the life of Colonel Hutchinson, 1904 edition, pp. 147–8
6 *Special Passages and Certain Information*, 28 February – 7 March
7 Heylyn, A briefe Relation of the remarkable occurrences in the Northern parts: viz. The Landing of the Queen's Majestie in the Bay of Burlington: And the repulse given into the Rebels at the Towne of Newark . . . (Copy in Bodleian Library)
8 *Hutchinson*, pp. 147–8
9 Master John Shaw secured the return to Hull of 'the great gun . . . which they had fecht thence to the siege' after the surrender of Newark. See *Yorkshire Diaries and autobiographies in the 17th and 18th Centuries*, ed. Jackson (Surtees Society)
10 *Collection of Authentic Documents* gives 4000 foot and nearly 2000 horse, *Hutchinson* 7000 collectively; *Weekly Account* 31 January–7 February 1644, 5000 foot and 2000 horse
11 *Mercurius Aulicus*, 16 March
12 Bury in *A brief relation of the Siege of Newark*, 1644, and Twentyman both state this fact
13 Thornhagh himself fought gallantly. Bury speaks of 'the noble and valiant Colonel Thorney.' *Hutchinson*, 'he fought very gallantly' with 'a great deal of honour'
14 *Newark on Trent: The Civil War Siegeworks* (Royal Commission on Historical Monuments), p. 19
15 *Ibid*
16 Sir Edward Walker *Historical Discourses*; Clarendon also commented (Vol. 4, p. 262) 'a very doleful entering . . . into the year 1644 [it] altered the whole scheme of the Kings Councils'
17 Brown, Vol. 2, p. 95, Slingsby in his Diary also refers to the fortifications
18 Thornton, *Antiquities of Nottinghamshire*, 1667, p. 198

[19] For illustrations and descriptions of all remains see Royal Commission on Historical Monuments

[20] *Moderate Intelligencer*, 5–12 March

[21] *Moderate Intelligencer*, 19–26 March

[22] *Hutchinson*, p. 284

[23] *Perfect Diurnall*, 6–13 April

[24] *Hutchinson*, p. 284

[25] While Brown (Vol. 2, p. 114) names the Mayor Smith, Twentyman calls him Baker

APPENDIX

STORM OF BRISTOL
26 July 1643

(De Gomme's Account, from JSAHR IV 1925)

Rupert's Army

It comprised 14 infantry regiments, "all very weak" divided into three Tertias. Lord Grandison was Colonel-General.

Grandison's Tertia

The Lord General's under Lt. Col. Herbert Lunsford
Lord Rivers under Lt. Col. John Boys
Lord Molyneux'
Sir Gilbert Gerards'
Sir Ralph Dutton's
Colonel John Owen's

Colonel Henry Wentworth's Tertia

Sir Jacob Astley's under Major Toby Bowes
Sir Edward Fitton's
Colonel Richard Herbert's under Major Edward Williams

Colonel John Belasyes' Tertia

John Belasyes'
Sir Edward Stradling's under Lt. Col. John Stradling
Colonel Henry Lunsford's
Colonel Charles Lloyd's under Lt. Col. Edward Tirwhitt

Cavalry

Sir Arthur Aston, Sgt. Major General of Horse, commanded the Right Wing
Colonel Charles Gerard, commanded the Left Wing
Sir Richard Crane commanded Prince Rupert's Troop of Life Guards
Colonel Henry Washington – 7 troops of dragoons
Sir Robert Howard – 2 troops of dragoons

Hertford's Western Army

Prince Maurice – Lt. Gen. Hopton – Field Marshal, Earl of Caernarvon –

Lt. Gen. of Horse; Earl of Crawford – Sergeant Major General of Horse; Colonel Joseph Wagstaffe – Major General of Foot.

Colonel Brutus Buck's Tertia

1. Marquis of Hertford's
2. Prince Maurice's
3. Brutus Buck's

Slanning's Tertia

1. Sir Nicholas Slanning's
2. Lord Mohun's
3. Colonel John Trevanion's

Bassett's Tertia

1. Sir Bevil Grenvile's*
2. William Godophin's

* He had been mortally wounded at Lansdown and the new colonel, presumably, was his fifteen-year-old son, John Grenvile, later first Earl of Bath.

RUPERT'S FORCE AT THE RELIEF OF NEWARK
21 March 1644

HORSE

Prince Rupert's troop of Lifeguards (Capt. Sir Richard Crane)	140
Prince Rupert's Regiment (Lt. Col. Dan O'Neale)	500
Colonel Charles Gerard's Troop	60
Colonel Richard Leveson's Regiment [1]	100
Major General George Porter's Brigade	1000
Lieut. General Lord Loughborough's Force	1500
Total:	3300

FOOT

Colonel Robert Broughton's Regt.[2] } Colonel Henry Tillier's Regt.[2] }	1000
Colonel Sir Fulke Huncke's Regt.[2]	120
Colonel Richard Leveson's Regt.	200
Major General Porter's Force	600
Lieut. General Lord Loughborough's Force	1200
Total:	3120[3]

LIST OF THE GARRISON OF BASING HOUSE
November 1644

Foot

Colonel:	John Paulet, Marquis of Winchester
Lt. Colonel:	Sir Robert Peake
Major:	John Cuffaud
1st Captain:	Peregrine Tasbury
2nd Captain:	William Payne
	Total: 200 foot

Colonel:	Sir Marmaduke Rawdon
Lt. Colonel:	Thomas Johnson (after his death Thomas Langley)
Major:	William Rowsewell
1st Captain:	Isaac Rowlett
2nd Captain:	Robert Amery (or Emery)
	Total: 200 foot

Horse

1st Troop:	Lieutenant Francis Cuffaud
2nd Troop:	Lieut. Colonel Sir Robert Peake
	Total: 100 foot

Thus the garrison at this time totals 500
Symonds B.M. Harleian MSS. 986

LIEUT. GENERAL OLIVER CROMWELL'S FORCE AT BASING HOUSE
14 October 1645

Colonel Thomas Sheffield's Regiment

The Colonel's Troop:	11 officers and 84 troopers
Captain Sheffield's Troop:	10 officers and 70 troopers
Captain Hagle's Troop:	10 officers and 70 troopers
Captain Flynne's Troop:	11 officers and 71 troopers
Captain Robotham's Troop:	9 officers and 63 troopers
Captain Wogan's Troop:	10 officers and 53 troopers
	Total: 61 officers and 414 troopers

[1] Garrison of Dudley Castle.
[2] Anglo-Irish.
[3] See 'Royalist Army at Newark', Major Peter Young, *Journal of the Society for Historical Research* XXX No. 124 (1952).

Colonel Montagu's Regiment

Lieut. Colonel Grimes
Major Kelsey
Captains: Blethen, Munney, Biscoe, Rogers, Wilks, Thomas, Disney and Sanders

Lieutenant General Oliver Cromwell's Regiment

Major Huntingdon

1st Captain: – Jenkins	3rd Captain: – Reynolds
2nd Captain: – Middleton	4th Captain: – Blackwell

In each troop 100 strong

Colonel Sir Hardress Waller's Regiment

Lieut. Colonel – Cottesworth
Major – Smith

1st Captain: – Howard	5th Captain: – Clark
2nd Captain: – Wade	6th Captain: – Thomas
3rd Captain: – Ashe	7th Captain: – Hodden
4th Captain: – Gorges	

Colonel Robert Hammond's Regiment

Lieut. Colonel Thomas Eure
Major – Sanders

Captain – Disney	Captain – Puckle
Captain – Charn	Captain – Stratton
Captain – Smith	Captain – Rolfe
Captain John Boyce	

Colonel Charles Fleetwood's Regiment

Major – Harrison

Captain – Coleman	Captain – Zauchy
Captain – Laughton	Captain – Howard

A LIST OF CHESHIRE FFORCES
(Add. MMS. 11331, 45)

Horse: Sir William Brereton's Owne troope under

Major Zanckey	100
Lt. Col. Michell Jones	70

	Col. Duckenfield	60
	Lt. Col. Chidley Coote	50
	Col. Brooke	50
	Capt. Hawkbridge	50
Staff:	Capt. Stones	100
	Capt. Vivers	50
	Capt. Shepley	60
Taken:	Capt. Bulkeley	70
	Capt. Glegge	40
	Capt. Collham } Capt. Edwards }	50
	Capt. Carter	40
		790

Foote

Tarvin	Sir Wm. Brereton's owne company under ye conduct of Lt. Col. Venables	150
Wirhall	Lt. Col. Cooke	100
Hooton		
Nantwich	Major Croxton	160
At Sall	Ld. Calvin Capt. about	100
Dragoon	Capt. Finch about	70
Salop	Capt. Sadler	70
Staffe	Capt. Monke	60
Wyre	Capt. Greene	120
Wirhall	Capt. Glegge now disposed of Capt. Birkened	160
Wyr	Capt. Rathbone	80
Tarvin	Capt. Hardware	60
Sallop	Capt. Spicere	40
Wirhall	Capt. Wm. and Capt. Rich Coventry and Capt. Ball	150
	Capt. Houltes Ffirelocks	1520

Dissolved	Adj. Louthanes Company Broxton hundred	80
	Col. Boothes Regt. (his owne compy under Major Daniell	70
	Lt. Col. Massyes	160
Country	Capt. Alcocke }	
Country	Capt. Grantham }	100
Salop	Capt. Geo Massey }	
Salop	Capt. Cartwright }	100
Both at	Capt. Whitney }	
Salop	Capt. Wright }	80
Nantwich under	Two Nantwich Comp[ies] of Townsmen Capt. Geo. and Capt. Thos. Mauberne	200
		710

Coll: His	Brookes his Regt. of ffoote own company under Major Church of Bucklow Hundred	140
Houghton Castle Bridge	Lt. Coll. Rich. Brooke	60
Strafford	Capt. John Brooke	70
Tarvin	Capt. Wm. Daniell	60
Nantwich both	Capt. Delves and Capt. Blomell of ye towne of Nantwich	160
Dissolved	Lt. Tutchets country company	80
		570

Colonel Duckenfield Regt.	
His own company	120
Capt. Boothes and Capt. Wattsones }	140
Capt. Sydall and Capt. Sellmerdine }	120
Capt. Smyth (Wm. Duckenfield erased)	60
	520

Collonell Mainwaireing his regiment

Capt. Leadbeater Cotton Baskerville Hancocke	About 160 all country men	160
	HORSE	790
	ffoote	4140
	IN TOTO	4930

EXTRACT FROM SYMONDS' DIARY
GARRISON in com. SALOP

K Tong Castle. First the King had it; then the rebells gott it; then Prince Rupert tooke it and putt in a garrison, who afterwards burnt it when he drew them out to the battaile of York.

K Longford Howse, the Earle of Shrewsbury. First the rebells made a garrison 1644, and held it till Prince Rupert tooke it at the same time as he did Tong Castle. Colonel Young is governor. Young's estate 300l. per annum, his wife a clothier's daughter.

K Lindsill, three myle from Newport, a howse of Sir Richard Leveson's. (Lindsill Abbey) Sir Richard L., made it himself, aboute hallowmas 1644, and still remaynes so pro Rege, 160 men in it. (He lives in the lodge). Bostock Governor obijt.

K High Arcall (Ercall), a howse belonging to the Lord Newport, made a garrison about the same time that the former was, made a garrison by my lord himselfe, 200 men in it. Captain Nicholas Arm[or]er is Governor.

R Wemme, a towne pro. Parl.; King, a Chandler in Chancery Lane, is Governour.

K (Blank) Castle, Sir Henry Fred. Thinne owes it.

R Morton Corbet Castle. [Col.] Sir Vincent Corbett owes it. Pro. Rebells. 4 myles from Shrewsbury.

R Shrewsbury, betrayed to the rebells in winter 1644. (1645).

K Bridgnorth Castle, [Col] Sir Lewis Kirke Governour: 300 foot.

K Ludlowe towne and castle [Col.] (PY.) Sir Michael Woodhowse.

K Stoake Castle, Captain Danet commands it under Woodhowse. (Lost in June following).

K Shraydon (Shrawardine) Castle. An Irishman under Sir William Ball (Vaughan) (P.Y.) commands it.

K Chirke Castle, Leift-Colonel Watts, Governour.
R A howse within three myles of Bridgnorth.

GARRISONS IN STAFFORDSHIRE

R Eggelshall Castle, 1644, 6 myles from Newport in Salop.
K Lichfield, Colonel Bagot, Governour.
R Stafford. Lewis Chadwicke, Governour.
R Russell Hall; a taylor, Governour.
R Mr. Gifford's howse at Chilleton (Chillington) three myles from Wolverhampton, now slighted by themselves.
K Dudley Castle, Colonel Leveson, whose estate and habitation is at Wolverhampton, is Governour.
R Tamworth Castle, four myles from Lichfield.
R Alveton, or Alton Castle, in the parish of A., about 40 or 50 in the Moorelands.
R Peynsley Howse, neare Cheddle (Cheadle) in Lee parish. Mr. Draycott, p. Reg. owes it. About 50 men in it.
R Caverswall Howse. Mr. Cradock, pro Rege, owes it. About 50 men in it. Captain Ashensurst is Governour whose father was a justice of the peace in Derbyshire.

GARRISONS IN CHESHIRE

K Chester. Lord Byron, Governour.
R Nantwich.
K Holt Castle.
K Harding Castle.
K Beeston Castle. Captain Vallet Governour, lord Byron's Captain. These garrisons shutt up by the rebells: Houghton Howse, Mr. Stanleyes, three myles distant from Chester; Puddington, Sir William Masseyes howse, three myles distant from Chester . . . Towne. These three are in the hundred of Worrall, com. Cestr.

GARRISONS IN DERBYSHIRE

R Derbye. [Col.] Sir John Gell is Governour. Five churches in it.
R Barton Howse. Mr. Merry owes it. Captain Barton, a clergyman, sometime chaplain to Sir Thomas Burdett, and Captain Grene-

wood, a skynner at Ashbourne in this county, are Governours. 700 horse.

R Bolsover Castle, the seate of the Marquis of Newcastle.

R Wingfield Manour.

R Welbeck Howse, belonging to the Marquis of Newcastle.

GARRISONS IN com. LEICESTER

R Leicester, the committee of Reb. governes; Theoph. Gray, third brother to the Earl of Kent, writes Governour: 600 men.

K Ashby-de-la-Zouch, Henry Hastings, Baron of Loughborough, Gov. The ancient seate of Hastings Earl of Huntingdon. 600 men.

R Cole Overton, a house of the Lord Beaumont's one myle from Ashby. Temple, Governour. 50 men.

R Bagworth House, or a lodge in a parke, the Lady Manors (Manners) howse; five myles from Ashby. 50 men.

R Kirkby Belhows (Belars), a howse belonging to Sir Erasmus Delefountayne. The men ran away at the newes of Sir Marm. Langdale, but came again. 50 men.

To all these garrisons above mentioned the yearly contribution amounted to fourscore and seaventeene thousand pounds, within this county of Leicester onlely. Of late Belvoir Castle has one hundred allotted to it out of this shire. And the whole number of men were not above 1500 in all these garrisons.

GARRISONS IN NORTHAMPTONSHIRE

R Northampton.

R Rockingham Castle. Sir John Norwich is governour, Lewis Lord Watson, Baron of R. owes it.

GARRISONS IN co. BUCKINGHAMSH.

R Newport Pagnell, also a garrison of the rebells.

GARRISONS IN WARWICKSHIRE

R Warwick.

R Coventree Citty. Barker Governour, a draper in the towne. Flower commands a troope there. A committee governes.

R Killingworth (Kenilworth) Castle.

R Edgburston (Edgbaston) Rowse, Mr. Middlemore's howse; the rogue Fox pulld downe the church to make the workes.

R Compton Howse, Purfrey son to Gam. Purfrey is Governour.

R Nutman's End. Mr. Chamblaines howse, of the Court of Wards.

R Rushin Hall. Fox G.

2,556l. 13s. 1d. ob. this was halfe of the part of fower hundred thousand pounds this county was taxed by them at London, toto 5,113l. 6s. 3d.

Every fortnight this sume is paid in contribution to those garrisons out of this shire.

The hundred of Knightloe in com. Warwicksh. paies every fortnight in contribucion 177l. 10. 11d.; to the garrisons of Warwick, Coventree, and Banbury; to Warwick halfe.

GARRISONS IN Com. MONMOUTH

K Monmouth. Sir Thomas Lunsford is Governour; Herb. Lunsford Governour.

K Ragland Castle, the habitation of the Marq. of Worcester. His fourth son Charles Lord Somerset is Governour. 300 foot. No contribution, and constantly paid.

K Abergaveny. Colonel James Prodgers is Governour; Charles Prodgers Leift-G.

K Chepstowe. Sir John Winter is Governour. The county payes for 500. 300 now in it.

K Newport. Colonel Herbert, first sone to the Lord Cherbury 50 men; contribution for 500.

GARRISONS IN GLAMORGANSHIRE

K Cardiffe; Sir T. Tyrell made governour by Generall Gerard. Sir Anthony Mauncell was first governour; killed at Newbery: William Mathew of St. Faggin's (Fagan's) Sir Nich. Kemys was governour when Gerard came, and putt out himselfe, and then Tyrel putt in.

K Swansey; Walter Thomas first governour; putt in by the King before Gerard came. Then Colonel Richard Connel was made by (blank).

This county never dealt with the militia. Never admitted.

GARRISONS IN ANGLESEY

K Beaumaris. Lord Bulkeley is Governour, Irish Baron. The King's castle.

GARRISONS com. DENBIGH.

K Denbigh Castle. Mr. Salisbury of that county is Governour; King made him Governour.

K Ruthyn Castle. Captain Sword, made by Prince Rupert, is Deputy-Governour under Colonel Marke Trevor. Sir Thomas Middleton did owe it.

K Chirke Castle. Captain Watts (knighted Sir John Watts 23.9.1645) –footnote. Governour; Lord Capell made him Governour.

K Holt Castle. Sir Richard Lloyd is Governour; King made him Governour.

GARRISONS IN FLINTSHIRE

K Harding (Hawarden) Castle. Sir William Neale is Governour; made by Prince Rupert. The Earle of Derbyes howse, and lived there sometimes.

K Rudland (Rhuddlan) Castle, two myle from St. Asaph. Gilbert Byron, (brother to the Lord Byron), is Governour, made by Lord Byron. The King's Castle.

K Flint Castle. Colonel Mostyn is Governour. The King's owne Castle.

GARRISONS IN MOUNTGOMERYSHIRE

R Mountgomery Castle. This castle was built by H 3 to prevent the rising of the Welchmen. (Holinshed, 6H.3, p. 203a).

R Red Castle. Hugh Price is Governour.

R Welchpole. Sir Thomas Middleton is Governour; Mason is, in his absence. Tho. Farrer horse (house?). Red Castle and Welchpole are within half a myle.

R Abermarghnant, a garrison made about the time the King marched from Hereford to Chester; 'tis Lewis Vaughan's howse, four myle from LlanVutlyn (Llanfyllin).

GARRISONS IN MERIONETHSHIRE

R Harley (Harlech) Castle. William Owen is now Governor, and is constable during life, and now sheriffe.

GARRISONS IN CAERNARVONSHIRE

K Conway Castle. Archbishop of Yorke was Governour, and Sir John Owen.

K Caernarvon Castle. John Bodwell is Governor. Only these two.

GARRISONS IN com. SALOP, 15 OCTOBER 1645

K Ludlow. [Col.] (P.Y.) Sir Michael Woodhowse Governour; quond. pag. o' Marq. Hamilton.

K Bridgnorth. (Col.) (P.Y.) Sir Lewis Kirke, Governour, Sir Thomas Woolrich was first Governour three years since; then Sir Lewis Kirke. 200 in the Castle. Leift-Governour Thomas Wyne, Sir Robert W. (Wynne's) son. Major Fr. Billingsby, jun., com. Salop.

K High Arcall, the howse of Sir Richard Newport, now Lord Newport. Armorer is Governour.

R Shrewsbury governed by a Committee

R Oswestree.

R Wemm. Major Bryan is Governour.

R Lindshall (Lilleshull) Abbey. Sir Richard Leveson owes it; Major Duckenfield lost it.

R Dawley Castle, seven myle from Bridgnorth, four myle from Wellington. Fouke is Governour; Duckenfield was and lost it.

R Bromcroft Castle. Mr. Lutley owes it., the Lord Calvyn Scotus is Governour.

R Benthall, Mr. B. howse, five myle from Bridgnorth. Thomas Brereton is Governour.

R Stokesay, a howse of the Lord Craven's, four myle from Ludlow.

A LIST OF THE GARRISONS OF MY LORD THE MARQUIS OF NEWCASTLE AND THE OFFICERS COMMANDING THEREIN NORTH OF THE RIVER TRENT

NORTHUMBERLAND

Newcastle upon Tyne	Sir John Mallory

Tynemouth Castle and Shields	Sir Thos. Riddall
Bishoprick of Durham	
Hartlepool	Lt. Col. Henry Lambton
Raby Castle	Sir William Saville
YORKSHIRE	
City of York	Sir Thos Glenham, and when he took the field; The Lord John Bellasyse.
Pomfret Castle	Collonel Mynn (2) Sir Jo Redman
Sheffield Castle	Major Baumont
Wortley Hall	Sir Francis Wortley
Tickhill Castle	Major Mountney
Doncaster	Sir Francis Fane
Sandal Castle	Captaine Bonivant
Skipton Castle	Sir John Mallory
Bolton Castle	Mr. Scroope
Helmsley Castle	Sir Jordan Crossland
Scarborough Castle and Town	Sir Hugh Chomley
Stamford Bridge	Collonel Galbreth (Galbraith)
Halifax	Sir Francis Mackworth
Tadcaster	Sir Gammaliel Dudley
Eyrmouth	Major Kaughton
CUMBERLAND	
City of Carlisle	Sir Philip Musgrave
Cockermouth	Collonel Kirby
NOTTINGHAMSHIRE	
Newark upon Trent	Sir John Henderson (2) Sir Philip Byron
Wyrton House	Collonel Rowland Hacker (2) Collonel Beeton
Shelford House	Collonel Philip Stanhop (Hope)
LINCOLNSHIRE	
City of Lincoln	Sir Francis Fane (2) Sir Perigrine Bartu.
Gainsborough	Collonel Saint George

Bollingbrook Castle	Lt. Colonell Chester
Belvoir Castle	Sir Gervaise Lucas
DERBYSHIRE	
Bolsover Castle	Collonel Muschamp
Wingfield Manor	Collonel Roger Moleneux
Scaly House	Lord Frenchville

General Bibliography

The Strengthening of Strongholds, Henry Ruse 1668.

Norman Castles in Britain, Derek Renn, Baker 1968.

Military Engineering During the Great Civil War, W. G. Ross. Professional Papers of the Corps of Royal Engineers, Vol. 13, 1887.

History of the Rebellion and Civil Wars in England, Edward Hyde, 1st Earl of Clarendon; best edition: W. D. Macray, Oxford, 1888.

The Gunners' Glasse, 1646. Wm. Eldred (B.M. Thomason Tracts E.371 (10)).

The Soldier's Grammar, Gervase Markham 1626, Second Edition 1627, Third Edition 1643.

Animadversions of Warre, Robert Ward 1639. Probably the most comprehensive on the art of war available at the time of the Civil War.

England's Parliamentarie-Chronicles, John Vicars. 4 Vols., 1643–46.

An Exact Method of . . . Fortifying Towns . . . and Defending Same, Thos. Venn 1672.

Anglia Redivia, Joshua Sprigge, 1647.

Index